Francis Delilez

The True Cause of Insanity Explained

The Terrible Experiences of an Insane

Francis Delilez

The True Cause of Insanity Explained
The Terrible Experiences of an Insane

ISBN/EAN: 9783337372491

Printed in Europe, USA, Canada, Australia, Japan

Cover: Foto ©Suzi / pixelio.de

More available books at **www.hansebooks.com**

THE TRUE CAUSE

— OF —

INSANITY EXPLAINED

— OR —

The Terrible Experiences of an Insane,

— RELATED BY HIMSELF. —

THE LIFE OF A PATIENT IN AN INSANE ASYLUM

BY A PATIENT

— OF THE —

NORTHERN WISCONSIN HOSPITAL

At Winnebago, Wis.

The Doctors of this Hospital, ignoring completely the immediate cause of Insanity, speak of this trouble as the Blind speak of colors, and are powerless to cure or even to relieve the Patients.

MINNEAPOLIS:

L. KIMBALL & CO., PRINTERS.

1888.

PREFACE.

Reader, I declare to you at the outset that I have been insane—crazy enough to kill. But in my misery, God has showed me what insanity is—its true cause and its effects. Therefore, to show to all as it has been revealed to me, what is the real cause of insanity, is the first object of this book.

The second object like unto it, is to show that generally the doctors cannot cure insanity, or even relieve the insane.

The third is to show how the poor insane are treated and maltreated in the hospital where I am confined.

The fourth is to explain to all what is the only reasonable treatment of the dreadful trouble and its cure.

And we believe that altogether will bring out the great thing we aim at—the relief of the suffering insane.

Let God, our Father, be our helper.

(Reader, don't skip the Introduction.)

THE AUTHOR.

CONTENTS.

INTRODUCTION.

CHAPTER I.

ATTACKS OF INSANITY.

CHAPTER II.

THE CRIME.

CHAPTER III.

IN THE HOSPITAL.

CHAPTER IV.

THE DEMONIAC'S WORKS.

CHAPTER V.

HIS SUFFERINGS AND CURE.

CHAPTER VI.

INSANITY AND THE DOCTORS.

INTRODUCTION.

Two great powers, invisible, spiritual, rule the world; God and Satan. Of course the second power is subjected to the first, for properly speaking there is only one Ruler of all things, which is God. Nevertheless the second power is possessed with great influence and ability, even working great wonders. In nature, in all the universe round about me, I see God. I see God in His works. And in all the wickedness and iniquities, crimes and miseries, I see in me, and all around me, I see Satan. I also see Satan in his work of sin and destruction.

From these external, visible things, I do appeal to the inmost feelings of every man and woman, and I say to all, you have felt yourself, yes, you, yourself, the influence of those two invisible powers. Oh! how many times you have felt the influence of the good spirit of God striving with you to lead you to do what is good and true, reasonable and charitable, pure and holy. And how many times have you felt also the infernal influence of the evil spirit tempting you to commit sin, rebel against God, and seeking to drag you down in misery and crime and darkness into hell. I know you have felt and feel those things in your heart, because I feel them in my own heart. And "the key of one heart, is the key which opens every heart."

But now, thanks be to God, we are not reduced to the necessity of judging on what we only believe to see and feel. No, because God, beside feeling and conscience, and beside the book of Nature, has given us another book— the book of Revelation, the Bible. Now, the Bible proves by itself to any fair minded person that it is the word of God, on account of the prophecies it contains. It proves that only the Spirit of the God who knows the past, pres· ent and future could so reveal those things thousands of years in advance. It takes a poor fool blinded by the devil not to see it, and not believe the Bible, be he lawyer, doctor, minister, theologian or layman. I know what it is. I have been myself a great infidel.

But more exactly, who is God and who is Satan? No man has ever seen God. But thank God, while man could not see God and live, God made himself a man. In Jesus Christ I see God, I contemplate God. "He that has seen Me hath seen the Father." "He is the express image of His person." "Before Abraham was I am." "Thou art my beloved Son in whom I am well pleased." The Lord Jesus Christ is the Word made flesh. And this Word, Jesus Christ, who created the world, came to redeem the world; and soon he shall come again to judge the world. Jesus Christ is the victim pre-ordained in the council of the Most High, before the foundation of the world to be slain for our sins, prefigured by the passover Lamb. Jesus, the God Man, was put to death by Satan, the enemy of God and men, according to the first and the greatest of all the prophecies. "And the Lord God said unto the serpent, because thou hast done this, thou art cursed. . . . .

"And I will put enmity between thee and the woman, and between thy seed and her seed; it shall bruise thy head, and thou shalt bruise his heel."

Now who is that old serpent? This old serpent is the devil and Satan, says God's word. And who is the devil and Satan? Satan was once, we see in the same Word, an angel of light, bright, beautiful, happy, holy, powerful. He got proud, rebelled against God, his Maker and Benefactor; he makes himself a devil. And he was cast down from heaven. He is now with his legions of demons on earth and in the air, active in doing evil. He is a wicked, malignant liar, subtle, deceitful, proud, and always a powerful being. He is the author of the fall, of evil and sin, misery and insanity. Such is the devil or Satan, a real, personal being, with millions of demons at his command, to help him in his infernal work of sin, death and destruction.

Now those two powers, declared by God himself to be irreconcilable enemies from the beginning, encountered each other nearly nineteen centuries ago in this world. There was enmity between the two. At the birth of Jesus, Satan tried to put Him to death by Herod. But kept by the power of God, Jesus became a man. A man like us in all things except sin. When a man Satan tempted Him to make Him fall in like manner as he had made fall all men since the creation of the first man. Here the Christ overcame the foe of man.

Satan left Him for a time, but he came again, and there was a struggle between those two powers, Christ and Satan, in that hour of the power of darkness. A struggle terrible, invisible, mortal. There was apparent triumph on one side. On the other there was a victory complete, decisive, eternal. "Having spoiled principalities and powers, Jesus made a shew of them openly, triumphing over

them on the cross." Yes, but the prince of life fell under
the blows of Him that hath the power over death in a cry
of anguish and love of all his soul! The earth is covered
with darkness! The light of the world goes down into
the grave! . . . . But the wicked one has but deceived himself. His triumph is but apparent. He has
bruised his heel only, and the seed of the woman has
bruised his head! The third day the Lord Jesus Christ
came victoriously out of the grave, conqueror of Satan, of
the world, of the flesh, and of death and hell! And His
victory is ours! Thanks be to God! "The God of peace
shall bruise Satan under your feet shortly."

But now, between the influence of those two invisible
powers exerted on our mental and moral nature stands
our WILL. We are free to choose to-day which one we
want to serve. But we have to serve one or the other.
We must serve God or Satan. "He that is not for me is
against me." "For as many as are led by the Spirit of
God are the sons of God." But "The power of the air is
the spirit that now worketh in the children of disobedi-
ence." Finally, "He that commiteth sin is of the devil."

Now when we have chosen to serve one of those two
masters, we are not free to do the things we wish. "Verily, verily, I say unto thee, when thou wast young, thou
girdedst thyself and walkedst whither thou wouldest, but
when thou shall be old, thou shalt stretch forth thy hands
and another shall gird thee and carry thee whither thou
wouldest not." That's it. If we choose to serve God,
God may require from us the sacrifice of our life for His
glory and our best good. But if we choose to serve Satan
(and we do choose to serve Satan if we don't come in
earnest to Christ to be delivered of his terrible bondage)
we don't know but next year, or next month, or next week,
perhaps to-morrow, the devil may arm our hand to kill our

neighbor, in a moment that he will have craftily bereaved us of reason by strong drink or otherwise.

Such is the condition of man. We are the slaves of the one of those two powers to whom we surrender to obey consciously or unconsciously.

But now I am going farther than this, and I boldly assert on the authority of the Scriptures that men and women may in certain cases at least, get so much under the influence of the Spirit of God, or more exactly, so filled of the Spirit as that the Spirit of God speaks directly through their mouth. That was the way at the day of Pentecost in Jerusalem, the apostles, all ignorant men of Galilee spoke the tongues of fifteen different nations that they had certainly not learned. "And they were all filled with the Holy Ghost, and began to speak with other tongues as the Spirit gave them utterance." In other words, the Spirit speaks through their mouth all those foreign languages according to those words: "For it is not ye that speak, but the Spirit of your Father which speaketh in you."

But now reader, and this is the point I want to make, in like manner that men and women may be filled with the Spirit of God so that the Spirit speaks directly through their mouth, men and women may be possessed of the evil spirit so that the demons act and speak through the possessed person. No fact is better attested in the Scripture than this one. For it is manifest (as some one has remarked) that the devil possessed and controlled some persons spoken of in the New Testament so that he acted and spoke through them, or made them act just as he pleased, so that all their actions were attributed directly to the devil and not to themselves. Yes, and we see that the Lord Jesus Christ, the Creator of the soul and mind and body, when He was speaking to some of those possessed of demons, spoke directly to the evil spirit: "What is thy name?" And the evil spirit by the mouth of the possessed man answered: "My name is Legion." In another place Jesus said to the evil spirit: "Hold thy peace and come out of him."

Those having the Spirit of God speaking through them are called the holy men of God. Those possessed of devils were called demoniacs. Now when we say that there were demoniacs, the doctrine is very ancient. It was fully accepted by the Jews and Gentiles before and a long time after Christ, but it is now a new doctrine as we boldly assert that in our time and generation there are demoniacs in very great numbers. In fact while God, the natural man, and Satan have not changed, since there were demoniacs eighteen hundred years ago, there are some to-day, while we live in the same dispensation. There is no way to escape this conclusion. Where are they? They are where we have seen them act and speak through the evil spirit that possessed them. They are in the insane hospitals. Therefore we hereby announce to all, rich and poor, high and low; learned and ignorant, doctors and patients, lawyers and clients, that all the insane of all the asylums of America and Europe, Asia and Australia, and all the insane of all the world, all, so many as they are, are demoniacs. And what renders them insane, mad, sot, crazy or lunatic is the evil spirit which possesses them. That's what insanity is. It is to have the mind troubled by the spirit of error and evil. It is Satan's spirit acting and speaking through the insane now as he did eighteen centuries ago. In short to be insane is to be demoniac. And to be demoniac is to be insane. Thus our doctrine of the real, immediate, effective cause of insanity is simple, simple. Wisdom comes from God. the uncreated wisdom, and is communicated to our mind by the Spirit of God. And folly, insanity comes from Satan, the author of all evil, and consequently of insanity, which is one of the greatest evils, and is communicated to our mind by the evil spirit. In fact, peace, order, harmony every-where are God's rules. And trouble, disturbance, disorder, are Satan's works. Now insanity is a trouble, a disturb-ance, a disorder of the mind: therefore it is produced by the evil spirit. Therefore such is our definition of in-sanity: INSANITY IS A DEMONIACAL POSSESSION.

Thus the person possessed of the evil spirit is a maniac, an insane. And the man filled, possessed of the Spirit of God is another kind of fool, of maniac. Said Paul: "I am fool for Christ sake." The two follies bear resemb-lance. Only one produces wickedness, crimes, misery. The other produces good works, joy and happiness. This one is the folly of God, it confounds the wisdom of the wise of this world.

We have not made this great discovery by our wisdom. In reading this present history of our troubles and misfor-tunes, the reader will see how God, our Father, has re-vealed to us this most important truth.

THE AUTHOR.

INSANITY,

Its Cause, Effects, Treatment and Cure.

CHAPTER I.

Attacks of Insanity.

It was in 1884. I lived on Dunbar's Addition to the city of Wausau. Wis. My next neighbor was Victor D——, my brother. In the spring of the same year my brother got sick. First he took care of himself, without improvement. Then he called to the doctors. The doctors could not help him. And the disease, an affection of the liver, they said, continuing its mortal progress, it became soon evident that the sick man was approaching the end more or less nigh. In the beginning of December, 1884, Dr. Kenouse, of Wausau, who was then taking care of the sick man declared to me, on inquiry, that in the present case death was but a matter of a short time, that death might occur in two or three weeks, perhaps in two or three days.

But a few days later, on the 10th of December, I think, about nine o'clock in the evening, the sick man made to his wife the strange declaration that some grievous and extraordinary things were going to happen, and told her to keep herself ready to call some assistance in case of necessity. And in fact, a little while after, the sick man had an attack of insanity more or less furious. He was

ready to strike her, though ordinarily he was a very quiet
and peaceful man. His wife, scared, ran to our house;
for up to this time the patient had kept all his presence of
mind. We went there. We found him sitting on his
bed. His gestures were disorderly and threatening. I
considered him for a few moments in silence, then I could
not refrain from weeping. I saw that exactly what I had
feared the most for myself or for some of my own ones—
insanity—had just happened to us. The sick man was
really seized with an attack of insanity. We immediately
sent for the doctor. Nevertheless this first attack did not
last long. A few minutes after, reason being returned,
the patient thought I was sufficient to take care of him.
He sent his wife and mine sleep in my house. Although
he remained that night in a state of mind restless and
feverish, the next day he completely recovered his reason
and enjoyed it for the eight following days, apparently so
at least. But it was evident that death was fast approaching. The sick man expected it. He made all the necessary
arrangements for the long departure, and he charged me to
bring back after his death his wife to her father's house
in Belgium. The 19th of December, in the afternoon, he
partook of the Lord's Supper with us, administered by
Rev. Margusson, of the Presbyterian church. That day,
it was Friday, the patient was very pale and feeble. In
the afternoon we thought he was to breathe his last. He
expressed his desire to see for a last time all our
friends and acquaintances. We immediately sent for
them. Those who could do so came during the afternoon, and the rest came until very late in the evening.
The patient received them all with an angelic meekness.
He had a good word for each one; very often a verse of
Scripture very appropriate. But as soon as the visitors
were retired into the next room, he was telling us that he

was in a great perplexity of spirit; that he saw himself on the grave's side with no assurance of salvation; that the promises of God which had so many times sustained and fortified him were now without effect for him. And he prayed. I prayed with him. It was then late in the night. The patient told us he was suffering intense moral anxieties. God, he said, had removed his face from him. The patient's face was of a mortal paleness, and considering him ready to die in such spirit's anxiety, I loved him in his misery as I never had done before. And his hand in my hand I told him: "My brother, oh! how I love you at this hour. Do you love us?" "I wish I could say I love you, he answered, but now I cannot love." And he prayed again. Then, on a subsequent inquiry, he replied: "No, I can't say I love you, I love no more, I am lost." . . . But my brother, said I, "you have believed in Jesus Christ, and it is written that He is the salvation of all that believe in Him." "Ah! yes," he said, "I thought I believed. I was mistaken. That was not the true faith. I am lost, lost." And after a pause he answered in a despairing tone: "No, no, I do not love you. The damned love not. I am damned."* But then the dying man commenced to pray with a novel fervor. He pleaded with God, reminding his promises of salvation in His Son. We heard him saying: "O Lord! I have trusted in Thee, I shall not be confounded forever." A few minutes later the patient cried out: "We have the victory. Glory, glory

*Reader,friend,don't you believe it happened here a very extraordinary thing to my brother. No, many, said Jesus, will say to me in that day, Lord, Lord, have we not prophesied in thy name? And in thy name have cast out the devils? And in thy name done many wonderful works, to whom it shall be answered: "Depart from me ye that work iniquity." This proves conclusively that many believe they are saved, while only lost, condemned in their sins. I know that once such was my experience. They are blinded by the god of this world. Let therefore those who stand in such deceitful security, get out of the snares of the devil, repent, forsake their sins and their folly, and seek earnestly the Lord while he may be found. The time comes fast when it will be everlastingly too late!

to the Lamb." And endowed at the same time as if with supernatural power, the dying man seated himself on his bed and declared to us that he had a revelation of the Holy Ghost to make unto us. And standing, he said, between heaven and earth, he requested us with all his might to listen to him; to resist him, he said, was resisting to the Holy Ghost, by which he was speaking. He requested us to fear God and follow him. Then he declared to some among us, the hidden deep evil of their heart. He told me that the Universalist's doctrine in which I then believed more or less, could be broken in pieces by a child that read his Bible. He told us th t François (the writer) should suffer a great deal. How the awful truth of that prediction has been fulfilled, the reader will see. After a long exhortation to all of us, he declared that he saw clearly that some of us would not follow his advice. (That has also proven to be too true.) He predicted several times that some great events were to happen, but that no harm should happen to his wife. Then he told us he had a vision, that he saw some great waters, and beyond the waters a wall, and beyond the wall a great multitude of souls. Then he suddenly exclaimed: "I see our mother—among them." He predicted also some other things. Some of them have already happened, and some not, and probably will not. He also declared that Satan has a great part in our diseases. Then in an effusion of love which has nothing in common with the earth, he exclaimed: "Ah! my friends, how they love in Heaven!" And animated himself by this love, he again requested all of us to persevere in the faith and do good. Then he embraced us, kissed a warm adieu to all, said he was pressed to remove, that he was going to die. He then laid down; he made a few long breathings, and all of us and himself, really believed that he was dying. He turned on his side and there he died—in his mind. He found himself passing the river of death, many were crossing the waters at the same time. And while many crossed them with terrible travail, he crossed them easily, leaning on Jesus. In fact, he had only died in his deceived mind, for a few minutes afterwards, his face so pale and white as it had been for over fifteen hours, became again suddenly of a yellowish color and ugly, and the dying man believed that he was cured, and said so, and asked for something to eat. Then suddenly in a new attack of insanity, he said to his wife: "Satan is there, there, you must cast him out." And his wife, fearing, trembling, exclaimed: "Lord do cast out Satan." But at the same instant, endowed with I don't know what strength, he jumped off the bed, seized his wife by the arm—but did not hurt her—he only set her out in the kitchen, saying: "Is it so my daughter that thou didst cast out Satan? It is in the name of Jesus Christ that one cast out Satan." We set him back in his bed. It was then about 4 o'clock in the morning. The doctor came. He said that because the patient's liver was diseased, a certain acid remained in the blood which caused the brain derangement; and after examination he found that the patient could live but two days, four at the most. But after breakfast the patient exclaimed again: "Satan is there." (He showed the place about the stove.) And he implored us to cast him out. Although we did not much believe what he was saying, nevertheless at his pressing request we fell on our knees and prayed God to help us, and the patient seeing Satan no more, was appeased. But a few minutes after he saw Satan re-appear, he said, and requested us with the most pressing entreaties, to pray God to cast him out, and this happened four or five times in succession. Then once after this, not having assented quickly enough to fall on our knees at his most pressing request, he again suddenly jumped off the bed, with a face yellow and awful to regard, and having some froth at the mouth, and exclaimed in a heart-rending tone of trouble and despair, "I am a demoniac!" I needed the help of the two women to put him back in his bed.

Reader, it is here the patient who for about fifteen hours has remained in a state of weakness between life and death. What is this? Insanity will you answer me? Yes, that's it. But what is insanity? that's the question. Well, the patient has declared himself in a lamentable tone, what was the cause of the trouble that tortured him, expressly saying, "I am a demoniac," and he is so well convinced of the fact that a few hours after, then again calm and reasonable, he told his wife: "François (the writer) will believe now that there are demons." And to me he said in a tone of firm conviction: "François, when I tell you that Satan is there, he *is* there, you must believe me." Thus was this patient convinced that insanity is nothing else but a demoniacal possession. Now reader, what was it the patient saw when he exclaimed, "Satan is there, there," showing the spot? I do not know exactly. But it is clear to me that he saw some representation of the evil spirit, Satan under one form or another. Was it visions, real visions he had at the time, or hallucinations? I don't exactly know which. At any rate we believe that the visions, delusions and hallucinations of the insane are brought about by the evil spirit. The devil is not dead, he is still living and working; be sure of it.

After he was calmed, the patient had already asked his wife several times what had happened the previous night. He had a confused remembrance that he had spoken and saw great things, but he did not recollect them. And as he was questioning us again anxiously about that in the

afternoon, I commenced to tell to the friends present the
patient's revelation and vision of the previous night. and
as soon as I related them, he remembered having told and
seen these things himself. He spoke of them ration-
ally to us, and even if I forgot something, he or my
brother-in-law, who had heard all of it, told it right. And
when I got through telling those things, I said to the
listeners, "Those are the things which the patient told and
saw last night; but my friends. you should not be surprised should you in a little while see the patient jumping
off his bed in an attack of madness;" and as soon as the
words were uttered the patient jumped off the bed, the
face yellowed again in an instant in an attack of delirious
insanity. Well, truly, if it is an acid that causes this
folly, it is an acid which seems very well to understand
what one says, at least.

When the patient was put back in his bed, we offered
a prayer to God. Then in a moment of great excitement
we cried out in clapping our hands: "It is Christ, it is
Christ who has paid for our sins, when he was nailed on
the accursed wood of the cross." And in saying this aloud,
the eyes closed. it came to pass that I suddenly saw a vision, oh! beautiful vision! I saw first some fire, then a
mountain covered up with a vapor of smoke, on the top of
the mountain a well drawn cross, and the blood was running abundantly down the cross, and in seeing this I told
my wife, "I saw some fire, a mountain, a cross up on the
mount and the blood running down the cross." This vision has recalled many times to my mind old Joel's prophecy repeated by Peter at Jerusalem on the day of Pentecost: "And your young men shall see visions, and your
old men shall dream dreams . . . . And I will shew
wonders in heaven above and signs in the earth beneath,
blood and fire and vapor of smoke." Then we got nearer

the patient, we took one of his hands, his wife got hold
of his other hand, and suddenly it came to my mind,
which was also losing its equilibrium, that if it was good
for us to get hold of the patient's hand, that it would be
good also for others to get hold of him. And I told my
wife to take hold of the patient, then our boy, then
every one in the house to the number of eleven persons,
beside the patient; and while all those persons except one
got hold of him, the patient again sat down on his bed
himself and he uttered a long speech this time in an unknown tongue. In what tongue the sick man spoke, I
do not know. Certain it is that all he could speak was
the Walloon (a Belgian dialect) the French, and very little English, and at the time he spoke none of those languages, nor German either. It appears certain also that
he did not speak broken words not to be understood, but
only a language that no one of us knew, and that himself
had never learned nor heard. What had he said? A certain experience explained to me afterwards that he was
confessing his sins to the eternal God.

Now we believe it to be a fact that the patient had
spoken by a spirit when he made his revelation in French
and had his vision of the souls beyond the waters, and also
when he made his speech in an unknown tongue. So believed the persons who heard him. One of them told me
the next day that he thought he was attending a spiritu-
alistic sitting, and moreover, that, scared himself, he wished
a great deal he could escape from the room. The only
question then is to know whether the patient spoke through
the Spirit of God as he believed and declared himself, or if
he spoke and acted through the spirit of error and evil.
Well when the dying man sat suddenly on his bed to
prophesy great things and had a grand vision, we believe
that even here he acts through the evil spirit disguised as

an angel of light who pursued an object that he even reached viz., to render some one else crazy enough to kill.* He is a murderer from the beginning; and when the patient made his speech in an unknown tongue he was evidently out of his mind; and God's Spirit does not produce insanity, but the evil spirit does. Then when the poor patient jumped off his bed ready to commit some follies and acts of violence, Satan works here in him as in a rough and wrong-doing demoniac.

After the patient got through that speech I tried to show up how the Saviour, in a moment of unutterable anguish and love had given up the ghost on the cross. But overwhelmed by excitement and deep emotions, and striken at the same time as by a partial brain paralysis, we could not get through. And under the sway of a terrible anguish, we uttered some awful and prolonged cries, and this occurred several times. Now there is not only one insane. but two. My wife and her brother took me home. I got in bed. Dr. Kenouse was called. He came and declared after examination that there was nothing serious nor alarming in my condition. The pure and simple truth is that the doctor had before him a dangerously insane person, liable at any moment to become a raving maniac, but he does not see it. He prepared some medicine to soothe me, he said, then he retired. But be sure reader that one cannot soothe a trouble like this with a little medicine. The next day, Sunday, I behaved well all the day. That was the calm preceding the storm. About nine o'clock I got to bed. But what an awful night! I shall never forget it. My thoughts troubled me. It came to my mind that I would heal my brother

---

*In fact to have really believed at the time that the patient was speaking through the Holy Ghost, that surely helped much to develop my insanity. But now reader, do you see how Satan here imitates the great works of God's Spirit, consisting in revelations, visions and speaking of unknown tongues?

by faith in the Lord Jesus Christ the next day in presence of all the witnesses who got hold of him, while he spoke in an unknown tongue. After that I heard several times distinctly and it seemed in reality the sound of a trumpet in the air.* It seemed to me that the end of all things had come. During that night of mental storm, four times in succession we were seized of a shivering along the spinal cord, such as we had never felt before, and each time in direct answer to a certain request of ours addressed to the Lord Jesus Christ.

CHAPTER II.

THE CRIME.

The awful night is passing away, but the terrible day of woe which has separated me from my family, until now, is coming. When the morning came, impressed with the idea of curing my brother, I charged my wife to assemble all the witnesses spoken of in presence of whom I thought to certainly cure my brother. Another thought troubled me. I really believed that the end of all things had come, and that Jesus Christ was going to appear. And from time to time, I called the Christ to come until I was completely out of breath, saying: "Come, come, come" and suffered much therefrom. In short I was in a lamentable state of mind. My wife instead of assembling my witnesses, decided with her brother, to send for the doctor. (She did not know then that the

---

*We must state here that our wife has told us several times while visiting us at the Northern Wisconsin Hospital, where we have been transported, and where we now write these things, that during one night right after our separation, she heard even so, the roaring sound of several trumpets passing in the air above our house.

doctors know nothing about insanity. She knows it now.)
When I knew that I got mad about it, and in my insanity
I got so far as to slap her. I believed I must necessarily
get her to obey me since I wanted to do the best deed
in the world—cure my dying brother. Dr. Kenouse
came. I received him very gruffly, unlike myself. I refused his medicine; and told him that absolutely he knew
nothing about my case. Here the mad man uttered a
great truth! For the doctor left me once more, saying to
my brother-in-law that there was no danger about me.
This, my brother-in-law has told me time and again, and
repeated to me after my return to Wausau from the hospital. The afternoon came. I took the Bible and sat
now beside my wife in perfect accord. I read the three or
four last chapters of St. John's Revelation. Then it
seemed to me that all things were so easy to understand
that I laughed at it. But then completely out of myself,
and seized with an attack of furious insanity, mixed up
with an involuntary rage, took an empty plate from the
table and violently threw it down on the floor. Then I seized
two books, one after the other from the table and so
threw them down, and then the Bible. And mad, furious, raging, I commenced to slap violently my wife. She
escaped and fled; I caught her out doors, and holding her
with one hand, I was striking her with the other. And
at the moment she was probably going to fall under the
violence of my savage blows, which fell on her as thick
as rain, and as heavy as iron, John Detienne, one of our
friends (as sent of God just now) ran to her assistance,
and came happily to snatch her out of my hands. But
now unfortunately she ran in the direction of my brother's house. I pursued her. But arrived at my brother's
house, I forgot her entirely and went to enter at my
brother's. And as the door resisted me, I seized an old

axe just beside the door, and struck the door to get it open.
Those inside relaxed their hold. I entered in; I passed by
my sister-in-law, the dying man's wife, and Ely Detienne,
brother of John, I looked at them they said, but I do not
remember to have seen them there. I entered the dying
man's room, my axe in my hand. I thought no more
of striking him, than I think, reader, to strike you now.
But as I arrived near his bed, these words were suddenly brought to my mind: "He says that thou has
a bad breath, but it is he that has a bad breath." And
always furious, raging, right upon that suggestion, I
struck my brother in the forehead with that axe, and I
struck so many successive blows that he rolled out of his
bed, swimming in his blood. And when I saw him lying
on the floor, I thought I could raise him from the dead,
and I cried out, "Victor, Victor," really believing he was
going to rise. I thought I had committed the best deed
in the world and I cried out: "Christ is here, Christ is here."
Lo! I did not know I had the devil in me! I got out with
the idea that if any one wanted to hurt me, all Wausau
would come to deliver me. But while I was hollering
out, instead of this, the police came, who overcame me
with club blows on my head, bound me with some assistance and brought me into jail.

Thus, in a moment of nameless misfortune, perished
under the redoubled blows of a murderous axe, by my own
hands, the dear dying brother that I loved as myself, and
whom during all the time of his long sickness, I had but
tried to relieve and heal, as all who know us could testify.

Reader, friend, who has just read the awful recital of
the tragic death of our brother, I ask you, has ever one
seen a misfortune like our misfortune? This attack of
raging madness, during which I threw my books down,
struck my wife and assassinated my poor dying brother did

not last, it appears, much over ten minutes. After this moment of woe supreme, I was insane for three months and twenty days, and except in a single instance, I have never thought again of striking any one. It is therefore evident that if some generous friends had taken hold of us just at that moment, they would have saved me from committing that crime. They would have saved my name from the murderer stigma, and saved me from this long detention in the hospital after my recovery. And then what! if we added to this, that this Monday, the 22d of December, 1884, the day of the crime, is just the fourth day after which the doctor had pronounced that all the patient could live yet was two days more, four at the most. But we know that here is God's wisdom, to draw good from evil. He has drawn the salvation of the world from the most abominable crime—the murder of his Son.

Now what explanation can we give of this awful crime? Insanity shall you answer me? Yes, but once more, what is insanity? That is the question.

Well, let us now see about it, in cold blood and in our right mind again, thanks be to God. And before all, let us state right here, that so far as we can recollect, it seems certain to us that all we have done and said since we got the use of reason, (unless perhaps on certain few occasions, while under the influence of drink,) that we could always do or not do, tell or not tell, all we have done and told until Saturday, the 20th of December, 1884. But in the afternoon of that day for the first time in our life of forty-three years, it is certain that we have done and told some things independently of our will, moved by the spirit of folly. Then two days later, the 22d of December, during the afternoon, it is certain and beyond all possible doubt, that from the moment when we threw down our books until we were overcome and arrested by

the police, that for that small space of time at least, we
have lost, not all consciousness, but entirely the control
of ourself, and our will power, and we have acted being governed, moved by a power outside our control, striking, smashing. breaking in pieces, as do the unconscious
machine wheels set in motion by a power outside themselves that runs them.* Thus in examining seriously
what has happened, I see that I certainly have done and
said such things as it would have been for me impossible
to do in possession of my reason and will power. And
how? Well, it seemed most certain to us that for that
space of time of about ten or fifteen minutes, while we
had lost all control of ourself, that some power, conscious,
intelligent, was leading this tragedy, was moving us, striking by our hands while in complete possession of ourself.
And this power conscious, intelligent, who leads this hor-
rible tragedy can be but Satan's power, who is a murderer
from the beginning. Yes, and we may go further and
say that we believe that Satan had prepared all things for
the crime; that he had first led me to insanity. Then
caused my wife to run in that direction; that he had
caused the others to hold the door so that I needed an axe
to open it; caused the axe to be right there handy, and
finally that he, Satan himself, brought to my mind that
suggestion about my bad breath, on which I struck the
first blow. (For we must say, that in fact, on the previous days, my brother had complained much of my bad
breath while near him.) And why should I not believe that Satan had a hand in all this preparation for
the crime? Had he not prepared men and circumstances,
fire and wind and all things, to entirely bereave Job of all
his children, property and health?

*Almost two years after writing the above in the Northern Wisconsin Hos-
pital, I became aware that about the same state of mind may be produced
by the dark science of hypnotism or animal magnetism.

We may cite some cases of men having in like manner committed crimes while controlled by a power outside themselves, but we rather say, if our conclusion about the cause of this crime and cause and effects of insanity is ac-according to God's word, we are right. If not, we are wrong.

Let us then consult God's word about it.

"And they came over unto the other side of the sea, into the country of the Gadarenes. And when he was come out of the ship, immediately there met him out of the tombs a man with an unclean spirit who had his dwelling among the tombs, and no man could bind him, no, not with chains; because that he had been often bound with fetters and chains and the chains had been plucked asunder by him and the fetters broken in pieces; neither could any man tame him. And always night and day he was in the mountains and in the tombs, crying and cutting himself with stones. But when he saw Jesus afar off, he ran and worshipped him, and cried with a loud voice and said, 'What have I to do with Thee, Jesus, *thou* Son of the most high God, I adjure thee by God that thou torment me not.' (For He said unto him, 'Come out of the man thou unclean spirit.') And He asked him, 'What is thy name?' And he answered, saying, 'My name is Legion, for we are many.' And he besought Him much that he would not send them away out of the country. Now there was there nigh unto the mountains a great herd of swine feeding, and all the devils besought Him, saying, 'Send us into the swine that we may enter into them.' And forthwith Jesus gave them leave. And the unclean spirits went out and entered into the swine; and the herd ran violently down a steep place into the sea. (They were about two thousand.) and were choked in the sea. And they that fed the swine fled and told it in the city and in

the country. And they went out to see what it was that
was done. And they came to Jesus, and saw him that was
possessed with the devil and had the legion, sitting and
clothed, and in his right mind; and they were afraid. And
they that saw it told them how it befell to him that was
possessed with the devil, and *also* concerning the swine.
And they began to pray him to depart out of their coasts.
And when He was come into the ship, he that had been
possessed with the devil prayed Him that he might be
with Him. Howbeit, Jesus suffered him not, but saith
unto him, 'Go home to thy friends and tell them how great
things the Lord hath done for thee, and hath had compassion on thee.' And he departed, and began to publish in
Decapolis how great things Jesus had done for him. And
all *men* did marvel."

We have here before us a violent demoniac deprived of
reason and will power. He is insane, for it is written
that "always night and day he was in the mountains
and in the tombs, crying and cutting himself with
stones." He is deprived of will power. For it is
written that "he was driven of the devil into the wilder-
ness." (Luke VIII. 29.) The devil speaks and· acts
through this man. For we see that the devil himself
cried with a loud voice (through the mouth of the possessed man): "What have I to do with thee, Jesus, thou
Son of the Most High God? I abjure thee by God that
thou torment me not." And the evil spirit (through the
mouth of the demoniac) answered saying: "My name is
Legion." And likewise all the devils besought Jesus, saying, "Send us into the swine, that we may enter into
them." Now that the infallible remedy against insanity,
is to cast out the demons, which cause it. is self-evident.
Nevertheless, we take pleasure in repeating again: "And
they see him that was possessed with the devil, and had

the legion, sitting, and clothed, and in his right mind."
That's it. While possessed of demons, he was insane,
mad, violent, furious. When rid of his legion, they see
him "clothed and in his right mind." Glory be to God!
And when the demons who were in him entered into the
swine, "the herd ran violently down a steep place into
the sea."

Now we have seen that in that moment of woe, like
this demoniac of Gadara, we were deprived of reason and
will power.* Like him we were striking, smashing,
breaking in pieces by a power out of our control. Though
a man of very ordinary strength, at the moment of the
crime it took the force of four men to bind the writer,
after having thrown him down by several blows with a
club, stricken on his head. If he was a little more or less
strong than the demoniac of the Gadarenes who "plucked
asunder the chains and brake the fetters in pieces" this,
no doubt, makes no difference in the kind of disease,
(more exactly "trouble,") for it is evident, that the writer
at that moment, was also endued with a super-human
strength. Those who helped to bind him d clare it. Now
like the demoniac of Gadara it shall be shown that the
writer was cured, set back in his right mind, through the
word of Christ, while ready to die in the hands of the doctors. Glory to Jesus!

Now when the demoniac of the Gadarenes was healed,
"he departed, (at the command of Jesus) and began to
publish in Decapolis how great things Jesus had done for
him, and all *men* did marvel."

And we do hereby try to do likewise. Whether he was
a better preacher than I, this makes no difference either
in the spirit which moved him and me after recovery.

---

*We must state here, that it was only two years after having written for the
first time in the hospital the account of our crime, about as read above, that
we have compared it with the case of the demoniac of Gadara as it is now.

Delivered of my demons, and animated now by the Spirit
of Jesus, I wanted, like him to preach the name of Christ,
the great deliverer from the power of sin and Satan. And
"tell the great things that Jesus has done for me." Praise
the Lord.—From the above it appears now clear to all,
that insanity has now the same cause—Satan—and the
effects that it had eighteen hundred years ago. And that
our modern doctors have found the cause of insanity almost everywhere except where it is in fact—IN SATAN.

God bless the doctors, and give them light. They need it!

We will show further on that the same devil is, in
like manner, the immediate cause of epileptic fits.

Now a little while after we were overcome by the police,
this attack of raging madness ceased, and gave place to a
state of mind which much resembled drunkenness. On
our way to the jail, we thought we were passing through
Wausau, then through Green Bay. We thus arrived at
the jail. There we recognized the persons around us, and
answered some of their questions. They placed us in a
cell. There, our head became very near like the head of
a man drunken with wine.* (Now we had been then a
sober man for twelve years.) It only remained in us as
a vague feeling of an indefinable *malaise.* It seemed to
us that some unhappy event had taken place, but we
couldn't tell what it was. The idea of our brother's death
came then to our mind. I asked the prisoners around me
if it was true that I had killed my brother. One of them
answered, no. I was glad of it. But this state of mind
like drunkenness, passed soon away. And we sufficiently

*In reflecting afterwards about it, we found that the state of mind of a drunken man comes very near, in some respects, to the state of mind of the insane. Hence it is clear to us that the spirit who possesses the insane, is the same spirit of folly and wickedness, who acts in a drunken person. The fact that many drunkards get really insane is a proof of it. Then, what warning my friends, for the person addicted to drink, to know that when once drunken, he is also more or less under the control of the evil spirit. And what responsibility to make himself voluntarily a demoniac, be it only for two hours!

recovered our reason, to know that we had assassinated our beloved, dying brother, and comprehended all the intensity of our misfortune. A deep, heavy sorrow ensued. And immense need to have some one of our kinsfolk around us made itself felt. I prayed the jailor to send for my wife. He did so. My wife came a little while later, with the only child we had. She did her best to console me in my distress. She bowed her head on my breast, and wept with me until the jailor ordered her to leave the jail. That evening, Doctors Willie, father and son, of Wausau, came officially to examine us. As soon as they got through their examination, a spectator asked the doctors: "Is the prisoner insane?" And Dr. Willie, father replied: "To answer the question, we must draw our conclusion from the observations we have taken." From this answer, it appears evident that Drs. Willie had not seen clearly into the prisoner's mental state. For the man, whom they cannot pronounce sane or insane after a long and serious examination, is a most dangerous insane for three days already, and is doomed to stay insane for three months and twenty days more. No wonder about it. For we are going to demonstrate that the doctors, superintendent and assistants of this hospital ignore completely the true cause of insanity. That they speak of the trouble as the blind speak of colors, and are powerless to cure or relieve the patients. But are in no wise powerless to injure or kill them. Moreover, if there is yet some honesty in them, they may say, "Amen" to this.

But for just now let us state that we did not sleep that night. It seemed yet to us that the end of the world was near at hand, and that the Lord Jesus Christ was going to appear. The next morning under pretext, in our mind, to make my wife come up to my cell, whom we believed to be at the jail door, while in fact she was sick at home, we set ourself to strike violently with our hand on the cell's iron wall and we hurt much our hand. That day we had also the idea of raising our brother from the dead. And we believed we had the power to do it, by faith, should only the authorities bring us to our brother's house. But they brought us, that evening, to the M. & Lake Shore depot to take the train for Oshkosh.

CHAPTER III.

IN THE HOSPITAL.

We started on this evening train for Oshkosh, escorted by the Wausau sheriffs and having some iron manacles applied to hands and feet. We were angry at the sheriffs who were taking us away, instead of bringing us to our brother's house. On the train we preached to men to repent and be converted, being impressed with the idea that the end was nigh. Arrived at Oshkosh, while I thought to be comfortably lodged at the hotel, we were brought to jail and lodged therein on the floor. We confessed God all the night, making, we think, not a small noise. The next morning the Wausau sheriffs set us in a cutter to bring us to the Northern Wisconsin hospital at Winnebago, four miles north from Oshkosh. At the time we were far from knowing where we were going. It seems to us that on the way the sheriffs jested and jeered at us, and very excited, we were loosing our mind more and more. Before we arrived at the hospital we saw the earth pass away and all things removed as a book rolled up. And just before entering the hospital it was represented to us that a certain Wausau gentleman who claimed to be our friend was but a traitor in this respect. And strange to say, but true, so it was. On entering the hospital we were out of our mind in such a way that in passing through the office, then from one place to another, it was for us the kingdoms of this world with their glory passing before us. While they brought us through the hospital it seemed to us that being beyond time we floated in full eternity subjected to some immutable, irresistible laws which so held us that we were unable to ever get out of their terrible embrace. Afterwards, Dr. Pember, second assistant physician, told us in reality at the time we were seeking in our madness, to bite those around us. Of that, and a few other facts, on a few occasions, we had lost the remembrance of having done those things. But all the rest of the time, although insane enough to do lots of follies, we recall all, and we are hereby trying to make up the history of our three months and twenty days of insanity for the profit of all concerned, for we believe there is much useful instruction to be derived therefrom.

At any rate we recollect to have seen, while entering the hospital, Dr. Pember, and the then hospital druggist, L. Hektoen, and an attendant of ward 3 and 4 south. The doctor and the attendant appeared to us at the time as hard and wicked men. (I said so after to Dr. Pember.) And the druggist (This I never told the doctor.) appeared to me as a real prostitute housekeeper. And the hospital where we entered appeared to us as a sheer house of prostitution.* What there is of truth in this appearance of men and things to the mind of a demoniac, the reader will be able to judge hereafter to some extent in reading the rest of this work.

---

*In regard to that, we must state here that after we heard an epileptic patient, when he was recovering the power of speaking after his fits, was ballooing in the hospital with all his might. "Whore house, whore house." The attendant was beating him cruelly to get him to stop, but could not. Then after being recovered it came in fact to our notice that some among the female employes seemed anxious to show that chastity was not their favorite virtue.

At all events we have introduced the reader into the Northern Hospital, and we promise not to let him get out of it without having (God willing) shown him what this institution is, in its work and character and by what spirit it is managed, after having studied its managers in their words and deeds for a long time. This is a most necessary work to do, because the visitors are only blinded by all that is shown to them.

We were brought into ward 3 and 4 of the south wing, in which were the worse and most refractory insane males. Our iron manacles were taken off and replaced by some leathern handcuffs. We were brought into a bedroom of the hall longitudinal, and there strapped down on a chair by the attendants.

Reader, in our miserable state of mind, this room was for us a kind of hell. It really seemed to us that being beyond time, we were in reality in eternity. For us, our room was one of the cells of those condemned to eternal torment. And each condemned had a place according to his deeds. Until this day our faith in a God full of mercy had sustained and comforted us. But in this cell of hell, overwhelmed by the feeling that our fate was sealed for ever more, this feeling set us in a state of mind impossible to pray again. Even the souvenir of our beloved ones can no more reanimate our heart cold as marble. At this hour, for me, there is no more hope, no more Saviour. The time of probation is passed away. 'Tis too late. All is lost, lost forever and ever. We have the feeling that a just God exists, and that we bear the effects of his justice. Some diabolical apparitions appear without ceasing. They are as some vapor of smoke which slide along side the wall. Seized with horror, I try to flee away, but only alas! to realize that, being bound where I am, there is no means, no hope of ever getting out. That set me in a great despair. The two big pommels of the maple bed-stead appear to me as two small human faces. I see them moving, *piroting*, and hear them whistle. And to com-plete this state of horror, I see in front of me, standing out doors erect in the snow, Mary———the assassinated man's wife. Yes, it was really her, Mary, her head cov-ered with the same black hat, clothed with the same black dress and cloak that she used to wear on Sunday. I saw her there, with her countenance of ineffable sorrow, until night came. There she was, as if to recall my crime, and thus added her part of horror to my already awful situa-tion. Some time after when I had sufficiently recovered my sight and reason, I saw that where was standing my sister-in-law, there was a hose house. The illusion then was such, that the hose house was that day transformed. to my hallucinated sight, into a perfect resemblance of Mary. I also found out that the whistling of the two pommels' faces was done in reality by a patient seated in the hall.

In the evening the keeper removed me for the night into another room where was a crib bedstead,* in which we were put to sleep. But I did not sleep at all. This is the fourth night we spent without sleeping. The next morning (it was Christmas day) we got up in a pitiable condition. When we were dressed, they put on our hand cuffs, then strapped us down. Then a keeper came with my breakfast. To fill my cup of suffering I believed I must fast. After having eaten a little bread, I refused to eat and drink, and afflicted, miserable, I sunk my poor head on my breast, my eyes closed. But suddenly, I felt my head straightened up by a violent blow striken on my forehead by the keeper. That is the way they pity the afflicted and miserable in this house.

---

*A crib bed is a box in the form of a cradle, with a cover with two locks, in which they put to sleep the worst of the patients in this hospital.

When being a little calmed, they loosed me and let me go in the halls. But in the afternoon of the same day, a clamorous insanity returned, and we were strapped down anew in a bedroom. There we commenced to cry out after the pastor, and an elder of the Wausau Presbyterian church, to which we then belonged. Lo! we did not know where we were. We believed that the pastor and elder could hear us, and they would come, at our request, to deliver me, for I had the feeling that I was a prisoner somewhere, therefore believed that the best I could do was to cry out after them, and did so.

Reader, this may give us already a fair idea of what insanity and its effects are. The spirit of folly, which troubles the patient, is for him a spirit of error, of deception and blindness. He introduces some false ideas in the patient's mind, and the patient acts thereupon believing that his views are right. For in fact the evil spirit is so well incorporated, identified with the patient's mind, that the latter generally believes that the suggested idea is his own idea and views. There is here no great mystery. Any unconverted person acts, led captive by the devil, without, in most cases, being aware of the fact. Thus acts the evil spirit through the insane that he possesses. Even the acts of violence of the raving maniac which are regarded as spontaneous are not spontaneous. They are suggested acts. While mad, raging, I commenced to strike my wife, I struck her on the suggested idea, that she was not willing to consecrate a'l to God, and that I ought to thus oblige her to do it to save her. Then I went and struck my poor dying brother on the suggestion about bad breath spoken of. Only we must not lose sight of the fact that Satan acts on the insane from within and without as we will see hereafter.* Thus the insane is generally maniac or mel-

*After being liberated, having compared with the acts, feelings and experiences

ancholiac (and so forth) violent or meek, glad or sorry, according as he is laboring under ideas joyful or painful, hateful or charitable. And the truth is that the same patient may be all that, and more in a few weeks, sometimes, in a few days, even the same day. Thus the character of the idea under which actually labors the patient, in most cases,unmistakably determines the form or variety of insanity of the patient; consequently to diagnose and classify rightly the patients, the doctors should try to detect, so far as possible, what is that idea or ideas. But they don't do it. And they can't do it in the very few minutes that they spend every day in each ward. But they classify all the same! Now, no two patients are laboring under the same idea. Generally each patient has his different false views and ideas. The truth is then, that the same devil renders all the patients insane, acts and speaks through them, with more or less power and manifestations, aided with his legions of demons. But he produces an infinity of forms and varieties of insanity of which the doctors cannot keep track. And in view of those real, existing facts, the classification of the patients, as it is now made by the doctors,

---

of the hypnotized subjects, our hallucinations of sight and hearing, smelling and tasting, our sensations and shiverings, the loss at times of memory, and at times the great power of the same, our state of torpor, our inability at times to express ourself, and at times the power to utter astonishing truths, and that impulse more or less irresistible (which is no more nor less than to be moved by the evil spirit) which caused us to make the greatest follies, against our feelings, for which we were cruelly punished, and how once deprived of reason and will power, we smashed and killed as an unconscous machine, we are now convinced that the motor, the power which acts through the insane is the same which works in the hypnotized subjects and somnambulists. That the hypnotic sleep is produced and stopped by some human acts and gestures does make no difference. In many cases, insanity is also the result of physical ailments or causes and Satan acts just the same through all the insane. Moreover, God governs the world by some established natural laws. Why should not Satan's power be subjected to some physical laws and causes in some cases, at least? Thus belongs to the dark science of animal magnetism or hypnotism, the merit of creating, with Satan's help,artificial insanity. And we may add, epilepsy. For let us remember that Mesmer produced in his magnetized subjects, some convulsions of long duration, which agitated and tormented them, and also that many phenomena which took place around Mesmer baquet have never been and probably cannot be explained by simple natural causes.

with their blind and capricious science, can be nothing
else but a fraud, a sham, a delusion, as generally are their
treatment, and all their appliances to cure insanity. The
doctors must know this to be a fact. Let the most honest
among them declare it.—But to return. On the evening
of the same day the first attendant came into my room
with Dr. Pember, and on the attendant's advice (not the
doctor's) each one of them set his thumb behind one ear
of ours, and with the rest of the hand, they conjointly proceeded to a complete strangulation to stop my hallooing.
(I was seized at the time by a violent and delirious attack
of insanity.)   But my cries only stopped the very moment
they checked my breath by strangulation; and just as
soon as I could breathe again, my cries began anew, though
they had caused me sharp pains in strangling in that manner. When they loosed my throat, the attendant blamed
the doctor because he had not pressed enough on my neck.
In fact I felt that the attendant's hand (a big strong man)
was a great deal harder on my neck than the doctor's.
After this, no doctor's hand has ever pressed about my neck
to strangle me. But we may safely say, that the same attendant did more than ten times afterwards do this savage work
on me. As for us, thanks be to God, this is our last attack of violent insanity towards others. After this we
have been for three months and eighteen days crazy
enough to do lots of follies, at certain times we have gone
so far as to injure ourself and even try to commit suicide.
But from this day they could cuff us, kick, drag, thrash,
torture, drop us from four feet high, the head on the floor
etc., etc., as they have certainly done, but by the grace of
God, we have been able to suffer all this violent, cruel and
inhuman treatment, without ever thinking of retaliation,
but always forgiving them as doctors and employes may
testify if they want to. To this spirit of meekness and

mercy that God bestowed upon us, even in our folly, we
owe our recovery. For the least resentment manifested
after their punishments, would have caused more punishment, as I see it happens with other patients, and in such
case, most probably I would never have got out the hospital but by the door that leads to the cemetery.

Right after the strangulation, Dr. Pember pierced one
of my breasts and introduced therein a medicine called
hyosciamia, which they used in that way to calm, they
said, the violent or boisterous patients. But after four
experiments of that cruel treatment, I do not see that the
hyosciamia, infiltrated in the patient's flesh at the cost of
sharp pains, or the blows, or the best strangulation might
calm a violent patient. Lo! it is the mind which is affected. It is the mind they should try to relieve by a moral
treatment. But to torture the body to relieve the troubled mind, as they do here, does not this rather resemble
folly, to say the least?

The day following, being again a little calmed, we were
loosed and sent in the halls. And although in a very
poor state of mind yet, making not too disorderly noise we
staid therein a few days. It was during that time that we
made confession of our sins to God. And thereby understood afterwards, we think, that our brother's speech in an
unknown tongue was the confession of his sins to God.
Some sins committed twenty, thirty years or more before,
were recalled. And as they appear to us, in their detesta-
ble ugliness, we confessed them to God, in presence, we
thought, of all the universe, men and angels assembled.
But afterwards we found out that this confession had been
made, in reality, on a bench of ward 3 and 4, that probably no one had paid attention to it, except a French patient. It was also during those days that we received, in
the ward the first visit of Dr. R. M. Wigginton, superin-

tendent. He asked me for what reason I had committed
that crime. And I answered him, "I was controlled by a
power I could not control. I have killed my brother inspired by the Holy Ghost." The doctor indignant reproved
me sternly. Yes, but all insane I was, I felt, I knew that
very moment, that Dr. Wigginton knew nothing about insanity. The answer I gave at the time to Dr. Pember confirms this: "What do you know about it, you, "*Science
of earth*" said I, while he spoke to me about my mental
state.

Now reader, remember that the insane in the time of
Christ, all insane as they are, had however some knowledge by the spirit that possessed them, that the rest of the
people had not. They knew and confessed loudly that
Jesus was the Son of God, while in fact generally the rest
of the people knew it not. It is so to-day. The insane,
all insane they are, possessed some knowledge which sane
persons have not. It is a fact that while insane, I came
to the knowledge of things that I had never known while
sane. And now believe this, it is largely what renders
some insane so stubborn in their rebellion against the employes. It is because all insane they are, they perceive
nevertheless that doctors and keepers know nothing about
their trouble. And here they are right. Among some instances in proof of the above statement, we will cite: I
have heard a certain patient who had so well understood the
real value of this hospital as a curative institution that he
cried out in and out of doors, "It is not here the place to
heal but to get crazy; humbug! humbug!" But who would
have believed that he was proclaiming a great truth! Just
as the one of old who cried out: "I know thee who thou
art; thou art the Holy One of God."

After having been those few days loosed in the halls,
one day it came to our troubled mind that our wife and

boy were with us in the hospital. And actuated by an intense desire to see them, I laid down on the floor in my folly, both arms stretched out, and I commenced to halloo, calling them by their names, "Catherine, Isaac, Catherine, Isaac." But while I was so calling my loved ones, lo! an attendant came who kicked me a blow on the stomach, as one would kick a savage beast. As the blow was applied on the breast bone, the bone sustained the shock and there was no fracture. Otherwise a poor patient of this ward told me that he had once two ribs broken by a kick of another attendant who is here yet. At same time another attendant came, and together they brought me into a room of the other hall and strapped me down there.

Now to be readily comprehended, we will call the first attendant the one who has strangled us with Dr. Pember. We will call the second attendant, the one who has struck us on the forehead, and third attendant, the one who has so kicked us on the stomach. Christ's law is my law. Its name is LOVE. The exposé we make here of the patient's treatment is done in behalf of the relief, deliverance, cure and salvation of the suffering insane. And in no wise to expose the employes cruelty, and the criminal consent of the managers of this house. May God help us in this good work.—And he does.

This attack of clamorous insanity lasted long. It seems to us that for three days and three nights we cried out at times. "Catherine, Isaac." really believing that they were in the building and would come to deliver me. It was the same idea that made me holler after the pastor and elder of the church.

The first evening of those three days of delirium, Dr. Pember, accompanied by the first attendant entered my bedroom and pierced the other breast to infiltrate therein another dose of hyosciamia.

But let us show by a fact, from among some others, how the evil spirit entertained in my mind the idea that my wife and boy were in the hospital. Among the patients, there is a demoniac who spent all the night in crying out, imitating a woman and child groaning, weeping under the pressure of great suffering. The illusion is here complete. In his groaning I really believed I heard the voices of my wife and boy. I believed they were suffering much at some distance from me. I suffer in seeing them suffer. And at times I got mad and tormented myself, because calling them instantly to come. they persisted in staying away from me. After those days of delirium. being calmed and loosed, I passed by the patient who groaned that way. He made at me a very significant gesture and called me by my christian name, "François," distinctly pronounced in Walloon. A certain time after this, while sitting very quietly to take our meal in the hall, by this patient. he uttered those two other names of some female friends of ours in Walloon, "Fine, Adele." This patient must be a German. Most probably he has never learned nor even heard speak Walloon. How can he pronounce those names in that language? I just see to this but one reasonable explanation, viz: This patient is a demoniac who utters those names, not of himself, but by the evil spirit. who possesses him, just as eighteen centuries ago the demoniacs spake through the evil spirit. Now in crying out all the night imitating my wife and boy—moved by the evil spirit—he confirms me in that delusion that troubles me the most at the time, and so fulfills Satan's purpose which is to make us suffer and drag us to death if possible.

Let us now state that while loosed in the halls, we had remarked, that when we thought of, or said something in a whisper, within ourself, and the most often in Walloon or French. the other patients answered right to what we were

thus saying or thinking of, by some gestures, some signs,
and sometimes also by their words.   Thus it came to pass,
for instance, that almost every time that I was making
such declaration as this: "All the promises of God shall
be fullfilled in Jesus Christ," that as soon as the words
were uttered within me, that one or several patients were
stamping the floor, or clapping their hands, as signs of
approbation of my words.   I then realized the very existence of a world of spirits, certainly invisible to human
sight, but which exists nevertheless.   In those days, I saw
almost as clearly as we can see anything else, the insane
acting and speaking through the spirit which possesses
them.   Thus was revealed to us the real, immediate, effective cause of insanity.   For we must say that after
those few days of delirious insanity in the hospital, we
then re-entered into a state of conciousness and reason
(though far from being recovered) so much that we generally knew and saw all that takes place in the ward, just
about as sane persons do.   During over two months we
behaved generally tolerably well most of the time.   During that time we were strapped down only four times, we
think, and only for the rest of the day, until we commenced our three last weeks of clamorous insanity, of
which we will speak in time and place.   For just now we
must state that during the first eight or nine days we were
in the hospital, we had the idea of having killed our
brother, inspired by the Holy Ghost, and of having committed a useful and commendable deed.   Now during all
those days, while in the halls, I heard a demoniac patient
who was saying almost constantly: "Murder, murder,
simple murder."   But after those days I recognized of myself, that I had committed a miserable crime, in a moment
of woe; that the Holy Ghost cannot inspire a man to kill
his brother against God's command, that said: "Thou

shalt not kill." And I tell you that the very morning
I recognized this within me, that same patient, who until
then had only looked at us with contempt, come and sat
by me, and said in touching sympathy: "You're all right.
You're all right." From this time he ceased to accuse me.

Not only was I seeing the other patients answer or ap-
prove what I thought of, very often. but also the demoniacs submitted themselves to me in the name of Jesus
Christ, or rather the spirit who possessed them caused them
seemingly to obey me. Listen: While I was either thinking of God or of his word, or praying within me, I saw
often one of them break into laughter so as to mock at
me, I thought. And I was telling him more or less in
whisper, and he sitting at a certain distance away: "You
must give glory to God." Sometimes he would let me repeat this several times, but then, many times, he not only
stopped laughing, but in answer to my words he acquiesced
by an affirmative sign of his head, which he always repeated enough to satisfy me. Moreover, once, this patient was coming to me in the hall, both of his fists closed
and raised in a threatening manner. And I told him:
"You must give glory to God through Jesus Christ."
And instantly he let fall his hands opened. Thus, and in
some other ways the demons seemingly submitted to me.
And I, poor fool, was very proud of it.

About the 9th of January, 1885, I wrote my wife and boy,
from whom I had been so suddenly separated, and whom I
had almost continually in my mind, besides all the rest.
My wife and some other parties, who have read that letter,
told me after my recovery it was a good letter. About ten
days later, we think, we wrote them a second letter. In
both of those letters, I invited them earnestly to come and
see me. My wife wrote to the doctor superintendent to ask
his permission to come and see me, but he refused to give it.

CHAPTER IV.

THE DEMONIAC'S WORKS.

All we have said concerning the demoniac's workings is very little compared to what follows. Listen: There is one patient who performs before me really some marvelous signs. He makes signs with his eyes, and he speaks. teaches and approves (shall I say?) with his hands and feet. This patient must be of English descent. I never heard him speak except in English. And he seemed to understand so well what I said within me, and in French or Walloon, that he answers me by signs and movements perfectly intelligible, and by some very significant gestures. Thus, if I consult him about some declaration, promise or doctrine of the Bible, he approves with his hands, sometimes with his eyes, signifying that the things are such without contradiction. While I am speaking, but always within me. if something escapes my memory, he scratches slowly his head with his fingers until I have found it. If I found myself in a very sad condition. where it seemed that God alone could help me. then he shows me the heavens, with his eyes. with a rare seeming of affection, as being the only place from which relief may come in my situation. But perhaps one of the fairest roles he plays, is when, for instance, I make a declaration like this: "And all those things shall be fulfilled to the glory of God the Father, Son and Holy Ghost, the only true God, eternally blest through Jesus Christ." Well, when I commence to make my declaration. within me, he at the same time commences to raise his feet from the floor high enough, and exactly at the moment I achieve it, he let his feet fall back on the floor. twisting them a little with an air of importance admirable to see, as in sign of approbation of my words. And those things and others, he executes almost every time I am speaking with him, that is, several times every day, during several weeks. Reader, at the sight of things so nice, so grand, so wonderful, a man (I really believed) who understood all I said in a whisper, in a tongue unknown to him, and answered it in my state of mind, I rejoiced exceedingly and thought that I had found a true prophet. For all those things are not delusions, they have really happened, and such we have seen them. Then I really believed he was the Christ, and I knelt down before him to worship him. And he, every time I knelt down before him, (this the attendants have well noticed) showed, by his attitude and gestures, that my worshipping was perfectly agreeable to him, and he always received it with marked pleasure. But one forenoon, the first attendant came, while we were on our knees before this new Christ, and he struck about four violent blows on my legs with a broom stick, which caused me to get up quickly, and he sent me into the next hall, warning me to come no more into this one. This ward three and four as two others of each wing are composed of two halls, one longitudinal with the center building, the other transversal. The two halls are separated by a door, which they only shut by night, so the patients of those wards go from one hall to the other almost at will, with rare exception. Now, so true it is that: "Though thou shouldst bray a fool in a mortar . . . . yet will not his foolishness depart from him," a few minutes after having tasted of the broom stick, I again passed the door to go in that hall. And as soon as I got over the threshold, this door between the two halls was violently shut after me, without being touched by any human hand. The third attendant saw it, and asked me who had thus shut the door, and I said "Nobody."

This is more than all that. One day I was preaching Christ, in a whisper, but this time in English. Such was my idea. I recited a sermon which I studied to preach to the unbelievers when I would be out of the hospital. First, I confounded the first category of unbelievers, who deny the fact of the coming of Jesus Christ on earth in saying: "But by what right do you deny the coming of Christ on earth, because you have not seen him? You have not seen either Alexander the Great, or Julius Cæsar, or even Napoleon the First, and lo! you believe that they have existed, by the recital you have heard of their lives. Now, do you not read in the bible, the testimonies of nine honest writers, who all declare having seen Jesus Christ, and his wonderful works, without referring to the multitude of prophets who have announced his coming? Well, the fact of the coming of Jesus Christ on earth, is a fact so well attested by these honest witnesses, beyond all reasonable doubt, that to reject the fact you must be a fool, a real subject fit for an insane asylum. And arrived just at this point of my discourse, a patient unbeliever, who denies the coming of Christ in the world, was cast down on the floor, unconscious, in convulsions, and it was a long time before he recovered. When he was set down again I got near him, and told him loudly: "Believe in Christ, believe in Christ." But the first attendant sent me away. Reader, I have repeated this same discourse about four times, at intervals of several days, and each time the same patient, when I reached this same point in my discourse, just as sure as I tell you, was cast down on the floor in his epileptic fits, or convulsions. The attendants have seen him laid down in his fits, and came around him. Only they have never known he was thus cast down at my preaching.

But listen: I pursued my discourse the first day I recited it, and then I addressed the class of infidels who do not deny the fact of the coming on earth of a man of the name of Jesus Christ, but deny that he was anything else than a wise, a great man. And to those I was showing up all their folly in saying: "But, my friends, Jesus Christ must be either the Son of the Almighty and Eternal God, or else he is not great, nor wise, for he gave himself out to be such. And when he was abjured, in the name of the Blessed God, to tell if he was the Christ, the Son of God, he answered: "I am, and ye shall see the Son of man sitting on the right hand of power, and coming in the clouds of heaven." Now in presence of these declarations of Jesus himself, there is no middle ground possible, you must accept that he is the Son of the eternally blessed God, or else that he is neither great, nor wise, but only a liar and an impostor.* And as I got through speaking those words, another patient stricken with convulsions fell on the floor. This one belonged to this second class of unbelievers, I think.

We continue our discourse, and we came to this third class of unbelievers so numerous, alas! in America and Europe, namely, those who believe that Jesus Christ is true God and true man, and despite serve Mammon and Satan in pleasing the world, and their flesh by fulfilling its lusts. And to those I said, as formerly Elijah the prophet, to the idolatrous Israelites: "If Jesus Christ is God, why do you not serve him and give him your heart? Why do you prostrate yourself before Mammon and give your heart to the goods and pleasures of this world? And just as soon as those words were uttered, (always within me) a third patient came out and stood before me. And

---

*But now to believe the humble and lowly Jesus, going from place to place doing good, and who submitted himself to the shameful death of the cross to do his Father's will, to be an impostor, is simply *demency*. There is no sense here at all. It is far more sensible to believe he was Divine.

far from falling on the floor as the two others, he resisted
me in the face. I tried to send him away in the name of
Jesus Christ, but he laughed at me. And while I continued to try to send him away, and he to resist, the first attendant interfered, and sent him in the other hall. This
patient is the very one who uttered those names in Walloon: "François, Fine, Adele."

A long time after those things, once, while I was again
preaching within me, I came in my discourse to the subject of Judas Iscariot, leaving the last supper table, to go
and sell his Master divine, and while I was remarking that
only a man possessed of the demon of avarice, could in
like manner, sell his brother, father or master for a few
miserable pieces of silver, behold! the very patient whom
I considered for a long time whether rightly or wrongly,
to be possessed of the demon of avarice, started at that very
moment to bleed at the nose. He lost a great quantity of
blood on the floor. The first attendant saw the blood,
wondered at it, and had it cleaned away by another patient. Another time some days after that, when I again
reached this same point in my discourse, and while I examined the crime of Judas in another aspect, this same
patient, has laid down on the floor, and groaned as if suffering much. Now during the five months and a half I
staid in that ward, I never saw before, nor after, this
patient thus bleed at the nose, or prostrated in like manner.

Now before going farther, let us see what mean
those things. For us they just mean this: First, this patient, this false Christ, who answers, speaks, teaches, and
approves by the signs and gestures of his eyes, hands and
feet, does not understand what I say. Yet, could he comprehend my French or Walloon, he could not hear me, because I speak within me But Satan, who understands
all languages and whisperings, knows what I say, and he

directs all the motions and signs of this demoniac. whom
he possesses, and makes perfectly connected with what I
say, or ask him. And that is the way. I believed that this
false Christ, heard and understood as God, all I said within me and in my language. Now I had come to this conclusion, when about seven months after my recovery, I
found in my bible these words explanative: "The man
who imitates the demon is a violent man, and his discourses are false. He makes signs with his eyes. Le speaks
with his feet, he teaches with his fingers. (Prov. VI, 12,
13.) * It seemed to us that those words revealed by the
Spirit of the One who knows all things from beginning
to end, settled definitely the question. According to this
word of God, written three thousand years ago, it is possible to meet a man who makes signs with his eyes, speaks
with his feet, and teaches with his fingers. And that is
exactly what we have seen. Only the scripture of truth
tells us, "That is a man of the demon and his discourses
are false." It is not safe to run after such a man. And
one will see into what a pit of misery, and suffering, we
have fallen after having listened to him, though not of
sound mind.

Now as for those who have been cast down on the floor,
smitten with convulsions, and the one who has bled and
prostrated himself, and all this just at the moment I condemned their belief or actions, in preaching within me, it is
impossible to adjudge such things to be the effects of chance.
But those unfortunates are demoniacs, lunatics, and Satan
who knows what I say cast down to the ground, smitten
with convulsions, or made bleed or prostrate, just at the
given moment, those unfortunates, whom he has in his
possession. Now reader, see how this interpretation agreed

---

*Literally translated from the Martin French Version of the Bible.
"L'homme qui imite le demon est un homme violent et ses discours sont faux.
Il fait signe de ses yeux, il parle de ses pieds, il enseigne de ses doights."

with the word of God, "Master, I beseech thee, look upon
my son; . . . Lo! a spirit taketh him and he suddenly
crieth out and it teareth him that he foameth again, and
bruising him, hardly departeth from him. . . . And Jesus
answering said, ... Bring thy son hither. And as he
was yet a coming, the devil threw him down, and tore him.
And Jesus rebuked the unclean spirit, and healed the child,
and delivered him again to his father." And again: "And
in the synagogue there was a man, which had a spirit of
an unclean devil and cried out with a loud voice, saying,
Let us alone; what have we to do with thee, thou Jesus of
Nazareth? Art thou come to destroy us? I know thee
who thou art; the Holy One of God. And Jesus rebuked
him, saying, hold thy peace, and come out of him. And
when the devil had thrown him in the midst, he came out of
him, and hurt him not." It results clearly from those two
passages, that the patient who falls with convulsion or
epileptic fits, foams, and staid there bruised, is thrown
down by the devil. The word of God coming thus confirms as completely, as exactly as possible, our interpretation of the patients thrown down on the floor, at some
given moments, by the power of the evil one. "There is
no new thing under the sun." No, what has been, is
what is to-day. Almost nineteen centuries ago some unfortunates were cast down on the ground, then violently
shaken, and foamed, and then remained there bruised for
a certain time. And now, nineteen centuries after, exactly the same things happen to the epileptic patients, in the
sight of employés and doctors of insane hospitals and
outside. The same trouble, with the same symptoms, is
exactly the same, and certainly produced by the same
cause—Satan—and all the inventions, conceptions or spec-
ulations of medical science cannot change those three beings: God, the human heart, and the devil. And while

those three beings have not and cannot be changed, it remains also true, that while the devil was rendering people insane, and causing their epileptic fits nineteen hundred years ago, he does the same to-day. Only those of our days having sought the cause elsewhere, there is a great difference in the treatment. Those of eighteen centuries ago, knowing the true cause of the trouble—the devil—brought their sons to Christ or the apostles—they cast out the devil, and they were cured. Those of our days bring their sons to the doctors of insane hospitals. The doctors give them some medicines, and other things, and cure them not. Who could put in the head of those doctors to attempt to cast out the devil with medicine? No one probably, but the devil himself, the father of lies and error.

Now, if some among our modern doctors believe that their science is too elevated to accept of this simple and true explanation of the real cause of insanity and epilepsy, Satan speaking and acting through the patient—we say to them: "But my friends, Luke, the Evangelist, was himself a doctor, for Paul calls him, "the beloved physician," and moreover was an inspired writer, and himself attributed positively in his inspired writings, insanity and epilepsy to the power of the devil, speaking and acting through the patient.

At any rate truth is truth. Whether the doctors accept or reject this doctrine, it is true nevertheless. Rejected truth is truth as well as adopted truth. Only the rejected truth profits nothing the one who rejects it. Christ died to save sinners; it is a great and blessed truth indeed. But it profits nothing those who neglect this only way of salvation.

But now so long as the sun, the moon and the stars shall shine in the firmament, so long as this earth shall stand on which we walk, nay, but rather as long as the everlasting word of God shall stand, it will be true, that Satan is the immediate cause of insanity and epilepsy, because the infallible word of God says so, and because Christ—the TRUTH—says so.

Now reader, friend, let me tell you, that we believe that Satan in doing those great works before us and at our command, pursues an object, that of making us suffer and die if possible. The truth is that like many poor sinners who serve Satan, I did not know it. I thought I was the happiest man. But let us always keep in mind. that, thanks be to Go l, the power of Satan is limited. He cannot torment us beyond the measure that God permits him to do, that the wicked one does a work which deceives himself, and also that "All things work together for good, to them that love God." But in the meantime, for us delivered up to Satan, we must suffer! Listen: When I saw that I could myself consult the demoniacs, that they submitted to me in the name of Jesus Christ, that the unbelievers were thrown down at my preaching, I got filled with great spiritual pride as one may conceive, in my state of mind.

Now let us state right here that for several years before our attack of insanity. there was another certain question on which I was not settled. This affair was a mystery to me. And just at the time as I considered every day Satan working in the insane of the ward, one evening this affair came right to my mind in my crib-bed, and forthwith I prayed to God that he would settle me on that very question. Reader, I tell you the things as they have happened to me in all this work. The next day, two demoniacs among the patients, showed me what was the matter about it, by their signs and their actions, and then even by their words, pronounced distinctly, I hearing them. And a few days after, I knew for certainty that the demoniacs

had informed me right on that question, their testimony
being confirmed by evident proofs which I received, and I
was forever fixed on that question. And in presence of
such a nice result, I set myself to observe and consult almost continually the demoniacs, really believing that they
would always inform me right. Here was my mistake
and my misfortune. For I know now that God has for-
bidden us to consult the spirits for our best good. Let
then any one who consults them through mediums, sooth-
sayers, clairvoyants, etc., take heed of it.

In the meantime assured by all I had seen and heard
confirming the fact that the insane are speaking and acting through the evil spirit which possesses them; one afternoon about the middle of February, 1885. I strongly declared to Dr. Pember in presence of the first attendant.
that all the insane, so many as they were, were demoniacs.
and if you want to cure them, I said, "Preach to them the
gospel of our Lord Jesus Christ, and as many of them as
will receive it shall be healed."

One day, we believed to do right, we ought to show how
the Christ has died for the salvation of sinners, thereupon
we laid down on the floor with both of our arms stretched
out squarely on each side of us. But the first and second
attendants came, they struck us badly to get us up. Then
each one of them took hold of one of our arms, to drag us
into the other hall. While they thus drag us away, I
earnestly urged them to go themselves to Christ to have
their sins forgiven. But the first attendant ordered to
loose me, and at his word, both of them loosed simultan-
eously my arms, and dropped my head down on the floor
from about four feet high. Then they picked me up, and
renewed several times the dropping operation—boldly
cruel I guarantee. They strapped me down into a bedroom of the other hall, and after that the first attendant

had beaten me severely, they went out and locked the door. Those things took place in presence of the patients of the ward. The cruel conduct of the attendants made indignant the most hardened. And one of the most educated of the patients, and the less insane, wrote a report of the affair and sent it to Dr. Supt. Wigginton. The doctor changed to another ward the patient reporter, and let those attendants remain in their place. About two months after, trying again thus to represent the sacrifice of the cross, the same two attendants beat me, took hold of me, dropped me several times in like manner, then strapped me down.

Twice, during the night, it happened to the writer, in a moment of impatient folly, to void the contents of the bladder and of the intestines in the bed. Both times he was taken, the next morning, into the bath room, washed, changed of under clothes, and then strapped down in a bed room. And the first time, as we made a great uproar, strapped down, in preaching, hallooing and stamping the floor, with our heel, Dr. Craig, first assistant physician came in, he pierced our right leg, and introduced in it a dose of hyosciamia to calm me. Now the truth is this: That very morning it had come in my troubled mind that those words spoken of Christ: "Thou shalt bruise his heel," had never been entirely fulfilled, and that a second Christ must come who ought to have his heels literally bruised. And counting myself to be this second Christ, I thus smote the floor to bruise voluntarily my heel to fulfill the prophecy. But now, reader, what in the world has Dr. Craig's hyosciamia, causing the sharpest pains, to do towards curing me of that delusion? No, it is evident that the trouble is mental, and it demands a moral treatment. The doctor's folly exceeds the patient's.

Once more at the start of our last attack of clamorous insanity (March 1885) Dr. Craig applied to us the hyosciamia; this time in our right arm. It did not calm me either, for that attack lasted three weeks.

Both of the times spoken of after the uproar of the forenoon, we fell into a singular state of torpor, though awake, and the eyes open. It seemed to us we were as in the place of the dead. Yet we could recognize persons, though all around us had more or less taken on a different aspect. The first time we saw on the walls of our room some small grasshoppers, and on the ceiling a bigger insect with long wings, flying from one place to another.

During our folly we have also felt ourself several times in such a state of mind depression that when we were speaking to some one in English, we began involuntarily to speak French or Walloon; then we commenced to speak English again, but like the drunken man, unable to keep our track, we spoke again to our hearer a language that he could not understand.

One day in February, 1885, we believed again that heaven and earth were going to pass away. And on the occasion we started to pray aloud after dinner. But the first attendant came and brought us into the next hall, and strapped us down there. Then in presence of something disagreeable we saw or believed seeing, we made some awful grimaces and screamed. The two other keepers came, they struck us, loosed us and brought us into a bedroom to be strap down there. And as we continued to scream, the third attendant kicked us violently several times on the stomach, to quiet us, he said. A little while after he left the hospital voluntarily, or involuntarily. I don't know which. When he left, a poor patient of the ward told me: "He is a wicked man."

In the meantime I wrote a third letter to my wife under the impression also, at the time, that the world was coming to an end, and that a new order of things was at hand to commence with the coming of Christ. And when I got through writing it, I was seized by so mighty a shivering that I was afraid of being raised up in the air from my bench. I prayed God that he will stop it, and a little while after, it ceased little by little.

Now let us say that the demoniacs, after having informed me rightly on the question spoken of, were now showing me every day that there were some disorders in my home, that my wife and boy behaved very badly. This caused me much intense moral suffering, which became more and more unbearable. In this circumstance, be sure, reader, that no doctor, no medicine, no human science could help me. Only one thing (humanly speaking) could help me, and deliver me from the delusion which overwhelmed me. See my wife, that she come and tell me herself that she loves me yet, and has not forsaken me. Right here was the remedy. The poor fool thought of it himself unconsciously. It was about the twentieth of February, 1885. I wrote a long letter to my wife in which I urged her to come instantly and see me: "Come, come quickly for it hasten to me to apply on your forehead burning with remorse and sorrow, the kiss of an eternal pardon; and on each one of your cheeks, the kiss of an everlasting love." Thus I terminated that letter. In reading it, my wife understood I had not regained my reason, but at the same time she comprehended my intense desire of seeing her, and immediately wrote to the doctor superintendent to ask his permission to come and see me. But alas! the science of the doctors of insane hospitals is too dry, too barren, too heartless to comprehend the wants of loving hearts! The doctor superintendent refused to let my wife come and see me under the pretext that her visit could but trouble and excite me. My experiences of

insanity authorize me to say, that, if the doctor means
here what he says, he is mistaken.   The truth is, that the
visit of my wife then could but re-assure me of her good
feelings towards me, disabuse, and calm me.   But now
that the doctor superintendent refused to let my wife come
and see me for my welfare, I am far from believing   One
thing is certain, viz: Since his admission in the hospital,
the patient writer, until then and long after, has been
treated and beaten therein as a savage beast.   Now, in
view of this fact, well known by the doctor superintendent, was it advantageous for him to give the patient, in
those conditions, an interview with his wife?   This much
we know: That the doctors of this hospital keep hidden
as far as possible, this cruel and inhuman treatment of
the patients.

At any rate, I was, by this cruel refusal, deprived of
the only human means of relief that it was then possible
to confer on me, in my lamentable state of mind.   But I
did not content myself with this refusal.   The next
month (March) I asked Dr. Craig to help me in the matter of having a visit from my wife.   He answered me, no.
A few days after I asked Dr. Wigginton to permit my
wife to come.   He answered negatively.   Then quite em-
bolding myself I told him: "Doctor, if you will not permit my wife to come for God's sake, as you are a husband
and father, let me see my wife for the sake of your wife
and children."   The doctor answered no, more or less indignant, and went away.

Now, by what lamentable abuse of authority is it possible, that the doctor superintendent of an insane hospital
in the freest republic of the world, may prevent a citizen,
confined in this house, for months, from seeing his wife
and children against their mutual wishes, and under the
most fallacious pretexts, after the light of christianity has

shone during nineteen centuries over the world, while 1800 years ago, a pagan governor of the most absolute monarchy, commanded expressly not to prevent visiting a Roman prisoner—Paul of Tarsus—any who wanted to see him, though he was accused of great crimes by those of his nation, I leave this question to be examined by all the honest jurisconsults of this country, who love their brethren and justice, and we beseech them, in the name of all that is pure, good, charitable and reasonable, to bring speedily about a change in this state of things. For the more they can seclude the insane from the outside world, naturally, the more wretchedly they may treat him.

Always more and more confirmed in that idea concerning my wife, by all I saw and heard through the demoniacs, I wrote her two more letters by which I earnestly invited her to come, and warning her of severe chastenings if she delayed any longer. Now all those letters were really written, received and read by my wife and some other people.

During that time once I saw a patient who really seemed busy with my own affairs. And I asked him, within me and away from him, what was the number of such culprits. And right away, he stamped hard the floor, once after another, to signify thereby the number he meant. And as he was making too much noise, the first keeper told him to keep still. And he answered: "I can't help it; I help a brother." Being several times after consulted by us in the same way, he answered me in like manner, and then gave the same answer to the keeper, when he ordered him to keep still. Some other patients have spoken several times to me (but without my applying to them) answering or speaking as rightly as possible to the things I thought of in my mind.

In the meantime we heard an old German patient, utter

distinctly, several times, and on d fferent occasions, those
two words, those two very names: "Jacko, Bebeth," that
I had heard fourteen years before, uttered many times by
my father-in-law and his children, on their farm near
Green Bay.   The first name had been given to a bird of
the blue jay species.   They had given the second name to
a milch cow.   During my three last weeks of folly, while
strapped down in a bedroom, this old patient for several
successive days showed me a place, at the foot of the bed,
by lifting up the mattress and blankets, and seemingly saying: "There, there is something."   But I could not understand his language.   After this, one evening. I saw
suddenly, at the place shown me, appearing a nice, big,
white hand with the wrist.   It manifested itself for a few
seconds, then disappeared.   At the time, I enjoyed much
reason in some respects.

At this time, one afternoon, I saw fallen on my clothes,
some small round things thin and very soft.   They were
surrounded by a black edge, with a white spot in the centre.
I picked up several of them.   I saw them also the next
forenoon in broad day light.

Once, a few days after my admission in the hospital, I
saw through the window, two small boys coming from the
west side towards the hospital, running and jumping on
the snow.   And suddenly I saw them disappearing as if
the earth had swallowed them up, and saw them no more.

Being then in the hospital about one month, I think,
one evening, after all noise had ceased in the ward, I heard
a voice calling loudly after me, quite seemingly from outside.   I listened. The voice continued calling my name
in Walloon, and urging me to go to him with the most
pressing entreaties saying: "François, come, come, will
you come?"   In the voice I perfectly recognize my late
brother Victor, speaking to me.   Sometimes the voice

stopped for a few seconds, then called again. And several times he added to my name, the name of my wife saying: "François, Catherine." The voice continued to call me thus to go to him most pressingly, and also in a threatening tone, for probably about ten minutes, then I heard nothing more.

About that time some awful dreams during the night frightened me very much. And one evening on entering my bedroom I said to re-assure myself: "But after all, they are going to lock thee up in thy crib-bed, and lock thy room door, no one can come and hurt thee herein." Then I got in bed. I offered a long prayer; then I slept. But while sleeping I was suddenly awakened by the painful pressure of something like a finger on my throat. As soon as I woke up. pressure and pain ceased, and this passage: "Wherever I may go thy hand shall seize me" came right to my mind.

But this is a singular vision. For two or three successive days. I saw, every time I went to a compartment of a window, in the sky. as six sword blades, with some gashes at the largest end, moving constantly in such a way. that sometimes they covered up themselves, so that only four of them were visible. But afterwards, they all re-appeared again. They had the color of the stars, and were perfectly visible in the blue sky.

But a more singular vision is the following: For several weeks, at almost any distance from them, I used to see, at the gas light. the faces of all the patients black. hideous, as the faces of reprobates. It was only when I got very near them, that their faces retook again their natural color. One face, among them all, was not only looking bright and white, but it shone as the face of an angel, at any distance away from me. That was the false Christ's face. Moreover, if one or several patients were near him, I saw their faces black and hideous, while the false Christ's shone beautifully. I told Dr. Pember about it after my recovery. He believed it, but did not try to explain it.

One day, I wanted again, to show up in the hall how the Christ had died on the cross to save sinners. But I hesitated in view of the punishment. And while I was deliberating to see, if I must do it, or not, to do right, at that moment, I saw a patient standing in the hall, immobile as a statue, with his arms stretched out squarely on each side of him. I took that for a certain sign, that I must then and there represent the sacrifice of Calvary. And I did so right away, for which deed I was beaten, dropped, and strapped down as previously said. Yet, it was certainly a suggested act, performed with the best intention on the part of the poor insane, as so many other acts of folly.

Once, I had in my mind that scriptural idea that Satan blinds the sinners. And lo! that day two of the most infidel among the patients, went to and fro, and even walked out doors with their eyes almost closed. The third attendant noticed the fact and asked them, I hearing it, "what was the matter with their eyes?"

During our attack of insanity our breath smelled very bad. In view of that repulsive breath, Dr. Pember, once ordered a tooth brush for me. And for a good while, I voluntarily cleaned carefully my mouth after each meal. But the breath did not improve therefrom. That did not come from the mouth, but from the stomach. It had commenced with our folly and disappeared with our recovery.

Once, one evening, I smelled a strange odor in my bedroom. The odor was not very disagreeable, but very strong. It seemed that all the atmosphere of the room was impregnated with that odor.

In the meantime, once, this passage came to my mind: "For they drank of that spiritual Rock that followed them. And that Rock was Christ." Then I got up and took a drink in the bath-room. And the water had a nice sugared taste. I had never drank such water in my life. The water tasted about so for some time after, then regained its usual taste.

But this is rather more curious. For a long time during our folly, when we spoke and prayed during a great part of the night, in a whisper, just when we happened to say something right to the point, in our judgment, we heard a certain shooting on the wall of our room, as if in approbation of our words. And many times we were answered right as the words were uttered by a noise— real noise—of water in our stomach, as one may hear sometimes in his abdomen. Then a long time after my recovery, I heard distinctly several times, in the middle of the night, a certain rapping, loud enough to be easily understood, in direct answer to what I said.

After my recovery, one evening, I heard in my bed-room a certain noise, as would be made by a small piece of money falling from the ceiling upon the floor. Then a crashing noise as would be made by the breaking of a strong glass. The next morning I looked around after the supposed piece of money. I found nothing. But I saw that a glass of my window was broken. I told about it that forenoon to Dr. Pember. He inquired to see how that glass, probably over twenty feet above the ground, had been broken. But he couldn't find out. Neither I.

And then, how many, many times, during several months, have I seen the other patients answer directly to what I said within myself, by their signs, gestures and even by their words, which proved to me then and now, beyond all possible doubt, that all the insane are animated

by the self-same evil spirit which possesses them, and
which directs all their deeds and words, to fulfill his infernal designs, just as the self-same good Spirit of God,
produces all the good gifts and works in all the children
of God, to accomplish his benevolent purposes.

I do believe now in spiritual manifestations simply because I have seen them; and the word of God confirms it.
"For there shall arise false Christs, and false prophets,
and shall shew great signs and wonders." Therefore we
see that those D. D's. and others who want to explain all
the manifestations of spiritualists and works of magnet-
izers, as though all were tricks, are simply unable to cope
with the evil. Satan is working there. And in like
manner do we know, now, that when the M. D's. want to
explain, as they do, all the visions, hearing, sensations,
etc. of the insane, as all mere delusions and hallucinations,
that they are here more deluded than the patients
themselves, because the patient knows positively, all insane as he is, that he has seen and heard some of those
things in fact and in reality. Only because he is insane,
generally the doctors and the laity do not believe him.
But the truth is, that the insane possess some knowledge
that the doctors have not.

Now in all we have seen, heard, felt. smelled, tasted,
proved, while insane, there are certainly some real signs
and visions seen, there is some real speaking heard, some
real sensations felt, etc. But it is also certain that there
is a great deal of mere hallucinations, illusions, and delusions. We will not attempt to classify them in this
small volume on account of space. Also it probably
would be a more or less useless work. Then it would be
very dangerous to make some mistakes. For though we
know that such are real things seen, heard, felt. etc., and
some others mere hallucinations and delusions, yet we are

far from sure we could rightly classify all of them.

The important thing here is to know that the visions, hallucinations and illusions, are purposely sent to the insane by the evil spirit, generally to confirm him in the false idea which causes his follies, or entertain such in his mind.

For instance the two things which contributed the most to lead us to the state of mind which brought about our misfortunes, were the hearing of the great things revealed by our insane brother, and our vision of the cross on the mountain.

When we believed ourself to be a second Christ, we had the most magnificent visions to confirm us in that idea. Yes, and once, one of the most *prominent* demoniacs kneeled down before me, his hands joined, in the most respectful manner. When we thought that heaven and earth were to pass away. we saw the sign of the sword blades in the sky and other signs.

When we believed that that patient was the Christ, we saw his face shine beautifully, while the faces of other patients appeared to us black and hideous, and many other signs of his supernatural power. And so on and on.

In conclusion, we may safely say that we know that without the signs and wonders we have seen and heard while insane, we wouldn't and couldn't have done a great part of our greatest follies.

Thus, Satan, the author of insanity, does entertain and propagate it. It is a great blessing now to know that such is the case.

CHAPTER V.

HIS SUFFERINGS AND CURE.

Let us now return to our adventures. It seemed to me that after I had myself asked all the doctors to have a visit from my wife, and invited her to come with the most pressing entreaties, that I had exhausted all the means within my reach. But I believed that my wife, outside and at liberty, had not done all she could do. I thought that if the doctor superintendent had refused to let her come, that she should have presented herself at the hospital office, nevertheless, and if the doctor refused to let her see me, then apply to the Governor of the state. And if this one refused to listen to her, carry her case even to the President of the United States, and I wrote her to do so. Now she had not done all this, and she had not come, and I must see her. I believed her guilty, and also the boy; and I wanted to see them, certainly not to chastise or curse them, but assuredly to forgive and bless them. Thus they would not come to me to be saved—and I could not let them be lost at any cost. What should I do? At this juncture, it came just to my troubled mind, that St. Paul to save the recalcitrant sinners delivered them to Satan for their best good, in order that the spirit should be saved in the day of the Lord Jesus. I resolved to do so with them, if however I found that such was the will of God. I had forsaken for a long time t e service of the new Christ. But now for a few days, having received by some new signs and visions, the assurance that he was indeed the Christ, come again there, and ready to manifest himself as the judge of the quick and dead, I had come back to his service with more zeal than ever before. Thus the first thing I did. was to communicate to him my intention of delivering my loved ones to Satan, and consult him about the matter. He fully approved my design. Therefore for two or three days I kept myself busy, in making in my mind a draft of the letter by which I delivered them up to Satan. according to an old custom of ours in writing letters and other articles. Thus the letter, more or less approximately as it has been written, had been composed and repeated lots of times in my mind, and as I tell you reader. almost every time that I came to the sentence of their condemnation, there were about three patients who approved of the deed by the most significant gestures. Beside, the false Christ approved it in his own way. and sometimes a fifth one also very noisily in stamping the floor. Deceived by those signs and wonders, I believed it was in reality God's will that I should write the letter and send it to them. In consequence—for those things are not dreams but realities—I asked Dr. Craig to let me write to my wife. And I then wrote the letter and sent it to her. The following are about the terms of their condemnation: "That they must come, (my wife and boy and two other persons) take me out of this house where I was suffering and detained on account of their faults, and bring me back to my house in Wausau, and if they had not come by such date, I delivered them up to Satan, in the name of the Father, Son, and Holy Ghost, the only one and true God."—Now listen: The letter being really written and sent away. while I thought of its contents in walking in the hall. I saw suddenly a patient, already spoken of, who seemed to be occupied with my own affairs, and forthwith I commenced to repeat. within me, the words by which I delivered my own ones to Satan. And at the same moment, lo. he crossed the ends of his legs in sign of approbation. When he had uncrossed them, I repeated the same words within me, and he, just like a soldier practicing, who obeys the commanding officer, crossed them again, and the exercise was repeated, three or four times in that way, perhaps more.   I took this as a ratification of the sentence pronounced against them, and I greatly rejoiced because I had found the true way to lead them back to me and their duties. But one day more reader, and myself, delivered up to Satan, instead of them, I am going to suffer mentally, morally and physically, probably, all that an insane person may suffer, and then die!   I say "and then die" because if we live yet, it is as by a kind of resurrection, surely.   Now reader, how many woes and grievous pains would probably have been spared me, had the doctor superintendent allowed me to see my wife, in time! for it is evident that it is this idea that my wife had forsaken me which led me into this present sad situation.   Now we had believed the victory won when we saw the sentence thus ratified.—It is no matter to wonder at to see us in our state of mind believing all the signs and wonders of those demoniacs as we have done.   Millions of persons nowadays, called spiritualists, claiming to be nothing but sane, really believe that all the communications they receive from evil spirits, come from their dead friends and receive those lies as truths.   God give them light, and save them too.

But the next day, after having passed a good review of the demoniac patients, who always confirmed the sentence, we passed into the next hall where the false Christ was. And after different signs of his power, believing in fact that he was the Christ, truly him seated there before us, we exclaimed aloud in French: "Father, glorify thy son, that thy son also may glorify thee."   And as soon as the words were uttered, that demoniac who had pronounced the names, François. Fine, Adele, although away from me started to sing. And the false Christ showed me how he answered to my words. Reader I assure you, that I repeated during that afternoon, from time to time, more than ten times, to say the least, the same words: "Father glorify etc." and every time we were thus answered by this patient or some one else, either by singing, or by some other signs. Thereupon I rejoiced exceedingly. But behold! all those signs are wrought in favor of error and evil, by the evil one to drag us to suffering and death! For it is the same evening, that our moral and physical anguish and sufferings were going to commence in a manner much more atrocious than ever before. In the evening I commenced to sing aloud in walking, and passing by the false Christ, who was brought back every evening in the hall transversal. The first attendant told me to hold my peace. I lowered my voice. But forthwith the question that we must obey God rather than men came to my mind, and I thought that if it was God's will I sing his praises aloud, that I must not keep still or sing low. Thereupon I resolved to sing aloud at any cost, if I only could know that such was God's will. Such are the thoughts and feelings with which we started, on the false Christ suggestion, those three last weeks of clamorous folly which have brought us to "two finguers" of the grave. I perfectly knew that to sing aloud while this attendant commanded me to keep still was to incur a punishment certain and severe. But I gazed at my prophet to consult him without saying a word. And as if he knew my intention, he showed me right away that I ought to raise my voice, by a sign of his eyes and forehead right up, the most intelligible. I started to sing aloud, but with trembling in view of the punishment. The same attendant told me sternly to keep still. But I believed I ought con-

tinue to sing aloud, and I did so.   The attendant mad
seized me and struck me.   I continued to sing.   He
brought me in the other hall by my bedroom; there he
threw me down on the floor and cruelly strangled me
unto complete suffocation.   Just so the devil treats the
epileptic patients!   Thus those keepers do exactly their
father's work! (John VIII, 44.)   Then he loosed my
throat, and set me in my crib-bed, with express threaten-
ings of more punishment if I sang again.   When I was a
little recovered of the pain caused by this cruel treatment,
I offered my prayer.   Then I thought seriously about what
I ought to do the next day.   I saw clearly that that way
of resistance, was the very way of the grave, and paved
with nameless, numberless sufferings.   I knew the merci-
less feelings of my keepers with respect to getting themselves obeyed, and I reasoned thereupon.   "Shall I," I
asked myself, continue to resist, and be killed by blows, or
shall I live in obedience as I have more or less done for
the past two months?   Terrible perspective!   Awful
dilemma!   Obey or be killed little by little.   But then had
not the Christ and many of his disciples preferred torture
and death rather than deny God?   Oh! what, what must I
do, said I! . . . .   Before I fell asleep, I resolved to
do what God wanted me to do.   To sing aloud and resist
even unto death if he willed, and to keep still if he willed.
The last I preferred greatly.   It was easier.   So resolved
I slept.—The next morning I got up fearing, trembling!
This question of life or death was again present to my
mind.   Again I asked, "shall I resist or submit?"   And
again I resolved to do at any cost what God wanted me to
do.   I dressed myself very quietly.   Then I went into
the wash room.   In stepping thereinto, I just saw the
false Christ, combing himself, his back turned towards
me.   And quite within me, I asked him if I ought to

sing aloud or keep still. And immediately he turned back, faced me, and showed me by an unmistakable sign of his lips that I ought to sing aloud. In view of such manifestation of his supernatural power, I fell down at his feet and worshipped him Two keepers came, they brought me into the hall longitudinal and strapped me down there.

Now the reader who would not have hitherto admitted our doctrine of the true cause of insanity, is, it seems, unless in some way prevented, compelled to admit it here. There is no way of escape. In fact, last night, while I rather wished to obey the keeper, it was visibly shown me that I must sing aloud. I did so, and was beaten and strangled on account of that idea suggested to me. I got up this morning greatly fearing the punishment. I desire to avoid it. But when it is visibly shown me in that supernatural way, I must sing aloud, I kneeled down and worshiped in singing aloud, him that showed me this. Therefore it is the false idea suggested to me which caused me to commit some follies against my feelings, for which I am grievously punished. Now that this idea is suggested to the patient's mind by the evil spirit, is incontestible in view of those two instances (without speaking of many and many others) of this false Christ urging me by some unmistakable signs to sing aloud against the keeper's command. I do not see what more palpable, convincing proof one could bring in support of a doctrine than what we bring here in support of the doctrine of the true cause of insanity, (viz: that generally this trouble is but the effect of one or more false ideas suggested to the patient's mind by the evil spirit.) except the authority of the word of God. But we have heretofore convinced the reader that the word of God attributes positively insanity and epilepsy to the power of the evil one, speaking and acting in the patient. Go now and cure this trouble with all the appliances employed in our insane hospitals. Would it not rather make one laugh to see those doctors puffed up in their science, attempt to cast out the devil with drugs, novels, dances, spectacles, card and checker plays. Just the means that Satan himself employs to keep people's hearts away from God. Without doubt it would be a matter to laugh at, should not alas! the application of those strange appliances for such a trouble, cost the people every year so many beautiful thousands of dollars, and specially were it not here a question of the health, liberty and life of our fellow men!!

A few days before the things we have just narrated, they had brought in our ward two unfortunates very far out of their mind. They strapped them down almost continually. The day I was rejoicing, one of those wretches strapped down, stretched himself on the two arms of the chair, and with one hand against the wall, he pushed violently against the strap, as if to break his body in two pieces. The false Christ showed me him doing that. Another patient loose laid his back across one of those chairs and let his head hang downward on the floor. This the false Christ showed me again. The next day when I was seized in the wash room, the attendants brought me in this hall and strapped me down just betwixt the false Christ and the poor wretch just spoken of. And a little while after I was bound there, I remembered to have seen the previous day those two patients doing those things, and that the prophet had showed me them acting that way. And I concluded he had thereby thaught me to do the same. And forthwith I started in fact to do exactly the same things. A new keeper, who had replaced the third attendant, came, and with the first attendant, they untied me, brought me into a bedroom and

strapped me down there, first by the middle of the body,
then they tied each one of my legs to the chair's fore feet,
so that I could hurt myself no more, except by knocking
my head against the wall behind me. And that I did. It
is worthy of notice how I started to injure myself again
by the false Christ's suggestion who had showed me the
previous day some patients doing those things. Now
while I was knocking my head against the wall, the first
attendant entered my room, and he struck me three violent successive kicks on the parts. Believing after what
had been showed me—see, reader, how the poor patient is
deceived—I ought rather let him kill me than submit myself to the keeper, I did not cease knocking my head on
the wall; but happily one of the most sensible patients
just then entered the room and the keeper stopped kicking me before him. Then both of them bound me more
closely on the restraining chair to prevent me from injur-
ing myself. But from those three violent and successive
kicks of a man as strong as a horse, struck on the testicles,
and so much more exposed to the violence of the blows,
that I had just the legs tied apart, there naturally ensued
some intestinal pains so violent, so acute, that I believed
this time my keeper had in fact given me the death blow,
and that I should die. But I looked at death rather as a
benefit and deliverance, in the lamentable circumstances
in which I was. And this house of woe and torture is
represented to the people, by its managers, as a home, a
residence for the insane! !

Nevertheless, the intestinal pains passed away little by
little, and a few hours later I started to sing the praises of
God strapped down, and I forgave the brutal keeper who
had administered to me so savage a remedy in my folly
and misfortune. During several successive days I sang
the praises of God, and preached Christ aloud, strapped

down, and very often I added to my song that the Christ come again down from heaven. was there seated in the end of the hall, under the name of Day Byrnes (which I pronounced "Barn.") I almost never ceased to preach or sing aloud, except to meditate, and pray. It was very tiresome for me to do that, I wished I could stop, but I was urged to sing aloud in different ways by the false Christ. But, very often when I stopped to meditate, in spite of all the signs and wonders that this prophet of woe had done before me. I nevertheless asked myself: But is that really the Christ? Is it certain that he in the hall, and I locked up in this room, that he hears me? In my doubts, I resorted to my visions. We had in the hospital, some visions so really grand and beautiful. that I regarded them as the glory of the Son of man. Generally in the middle of the vision was a spot, where was seen a small golden wheel fluttering without ceasing, and this wheel appeared and disappeared really at my word. it seemed to me. This was the vision I consulted. to confirm what the false Christ and the other demoniacs revealed to me. And altogether by their deceptions they have led me almost to the grave. But now strapped down in my room, if I had some doubt that that patient was the Christ. brought about by the attendants, who several times told me that he was only a murderer like me, (literally) or otherwise, I consulted my visions, and every time they responded that Day Byrnes was really the Christ. Several times also I answered the keepers: "But when I speak to him in a whisper and in my language he answers me, he has revealed himself to me as the Son of God." Also. lots of times, in fact, while loosed for some necessity, I faced him, and asked him, within me, if he was really the Christ, and every time, he answered by a good affirmative sign. Yes, and it is worthy of notice, that after being

completely recovered, I was going very often for my
pleasure and curiosity to look at this patient, always seated in the east end of the hall longitudinal, and every time,
as soon as he perceived me, this demoniac invited me by
the most entreating gestures to get me to worship him
again. He has done that as long as he remained in the
hospital.

In the meantime, as for us, our life had become most
miserable. I sang and preached almost all the day
long, strapped down in a bedroom, and when loosed,
generally, if I had the opportunity, I ran and kneeled
down before the false Christ, for which I received almost
every time some punishment more or less painful. In
fact, once for instance the new attendant spoken of, having found me kneeled down before him, gave me three
violent kicks right on the back of the neck. Several
times he striped me on the naked body with a heavy strap
for that offence. But worse is coming. For over two
months, I generally had taken my meals. But since those
last days of clamorous folly, I had already, several times,
refused to eat. Then one day in meditating on the life of
Christ I found he had fasted for forty days, and that I
ought to do so. Then I found also that to do the will of
God on earth as it is in heaven, I ought to sing his praises
day and night. I consulted my visions, and they approved
completely those two new plans, just what I needed to kill
myself, with the blows which were surely not spared me.
I then refused to eat. The keepers tormented me some, in
vain to make me eat. Then I was fed with a stomach
pump by the doctor. This was one more species of suffering. Then I also started to sing all the night. But I got
asleep in spite of me. The next evening I uncovered myself, and the cold preventing sleep, I could thus sing
about all the night. But the following evening, as I was

singing again, the night watch ordered me to keep still. I
told him I believed in conscience I ought to sing God's
praises. He ordered the second and third attendants to
lay hold of me, and after a desperate resistance, unheard
of on my part, he succeeded in making me swallow a glass-
ful of the abominable opiate, that they give in this hospital
to the noisy patients to quiet them during the night. The
next evening, as I was singing again, the nightwatch
came with the two same attendants and succeeded in getting me to take his repulsive narcotic, after the most ob-
stinate resistance, and the greatest sufferings on my part.
Lo! I believed that I must let myself be tortured rather
than take the opiate! And they tortured me night after
night, with an infernal persistence to make me take it!
One evening, after they had thus tortured me, when they
loosed me from their grasp, I told them: "You crucify
me, my brethren." They looked at each other and got
out of the room; but only to come back the following evening, animated by the same cruel feelings. God have
mercy upon their souls!! Listen, reader: To keep my
face still to make me take the opiate, the night watch had
pressed his thumb on my right cheek so that he had
bruised the flesh. And as a consequence of that bruise,
there came forth a grievous eruption, which the attendants, the doctor, and my wife, at the time of her first visit,
have seen. It took over three weeks to cure it. And in
pressing violently with the glass on my lower lip, to make
me open my mouth, he had smashed the flesh so as to
make it bleed inside of the mouth. Now with a face so
bruised, the last time he came to my room to give me the
narcotic, when he got ready to lay his hands on my face
to hold it still, I told the nightwatch: "Sir, see how you
have bruised my face for the last days." And he rejoined:
"If you will not stop singing I am going to hurt you now

again." And I told him: "I cannot promise you to stop, I obey my conscience, I sing the praises of God." The attendants in the meantime had taken hold of me. And the night watch thrust his thumb into the old cheek wound, and he violently pressed the glass containing the opiate. on the bruised lip. inside, unto blood. and after a few minutes of resistance, giving up under the pressure of atrocious pains, I loosed my teeth, and swallowed a part of the narcotic. Then I suddenly shook my head, and a part of the drug was spilled. The night watch ordered the two keepers not to release me, and right away he filled up the glass. then pressing with his thumb and the glass on the old wounds. he got my teeth open after an infuriated resistance on my part, under the pressure of excruciating pains, which make me scream as a roaring lion. And as the first time. again I suddenly shook my head, and a part of the opiate was spilled. And the nightwatch, equally determined, filled the glass again for the third time, and without waiting in the least, to see if I had swallowed enough or not of the opiate to quiet me, he forced me to take all the contents of this last third glass, after a resistance which cost me horrid pains, and made me scream awfully. Then he went away, leaving me to the care of the two attendants, who brought me into the bath-room to wash me. for I was all soiled after such atrocious struggles.

Now, I tell you reader that these things have in fact and in reality happened to me as above related, just before my recovery which took place on the 12th of April, 1885. Besides, in all this work, being actuated by the desire to tell the truth. how could I speak against it? Thus was the writer tortured day after day in this awful home of the state! ! It is evident that when the people send here their loved ones they don't know what they are doing.

Hence the urgent necessity to reveal to the people what takes place daily in this house of woe and torture. And so much the more as all those cruelties and tortures are inflicted on the insane without the least necessity. There is no reason for abusing the patients. When thus tortured to make me take the opiate, my tormentor told me that it was to quiet me in order that the other patients could sleep. Now mark, tired as I was, having already sang all the day long I used to sing much lower during the night, and perhaps such song would rather have influenced to sleep the other patients.

But this is not all. While thus tortured by night to make me take this chemical restraint, some other tortures were inflicted on us during the day time to make us take another medicine, which I refused also to take. On my refusal, the first attendant was ordering another attendant or patient to take hold of me, who reversed my head behind, downward; then they tried to force my mouth open to pour in the medicine. And when he could not succeed on account of my resistance, once, the first attendant poured this very strong medicine into my stomach little by little, by the nostrils. That naturally caused me some atrocious pains which lasted a long time after having taken it. And the keeper felicitated himself on his success before me, and after, he employed again the same means to make me take it. And now think of it. In feeding me with the stomach pump as they then did every day, they could have put my medicines in the liquid food, and thus get me to take it without trouble and without hurting me at all. If they had done that, and transported the false Christ into another ward, through those two easy, feasible means, they would have delivered me of the greatest of my troubles and sufferings. Surely, "It is not here the place to heal but to get crazy."

When recovered and taking then voluntarily the same medicine, this same attendant very often forgot to give it to me three times daily, as prescribed.

It is the diabolical principle to want the poor patient to submit to their will which makes those employes beat, strangle, kick, thrash, hurt, bruise, drop, torture the same patient rather than let him have his way. We have abundant proofs that it is this senseless, infernal principle which actuates those employes, but on account of space, we will only cite an example in support of our assertion. One day, during those three last weeks of folly, Dr. Craig ordered me loosed. The first attendant commanded me to stop in the hall longitudinal. But always actuated by that spirit of deception and resistance, I went into the other hall, against his order. And the keeper, mad, hastened to me, he seized me and brought me back into the hall where I came from, striking me violently with his heavy fist in my side and stomach. He hurt me severely. And in thus beating me, he said that it was because I had passed from one hall to the other against his command. Then he brought me back into one of the bedrooms and re-strapped me down there.—You hear it. The keeper declares it. He strikes me violently, cruelly, simply because the poor fool has broken his command, and with no other necessity than to gratify himself, and avenge his authority, disregarded by an insane! Now this attendant has been consecutively employed in this house for twelve or thirteen years, and receives the far highest salary. If he was not actuated by the principle which prevails in the government of this hospital, and in the general treatment of the patients, how could he have maintained himself so long in the service of this house!

Reader friend, once, one of Bonaparte's generals, sent by means of powder, up to the sky, the building of the

Tribunal of the Romish Inquisition of Spain, where they tortured the so-called heretics. That was not the right way to do business, I think. The building was rebuilt. But since that time, as a matter of fact, civilization has abolished torture in every civilized country, except in insane asylums. But here torture still exists, and is practiced on the insane. It has been practiced on the writer's body, and others. Now observe, that the same principle produces the same acts of violence in the two cases in question. Rome papal tortured the heretics so-called, to make them submit to her infallible authority (?)! And the employes of this hospital in like manner beat, strangle, torture the patients, to try to get them to submit to their arbitrary will! It belongs now to this generation to wipe torture and maltreatment out of insane hospitals.

But let us state that as for us, at present, we reason more or less well. And sometimes we astonish and confound our contradictors by our logical answers. Only we have a weak point, that of believing that that patient is the Christ. From this false fixed idea springs now all our follies. We are a confirmed monomaniac so-called, for just now, and one of the worst kind to heal, said a scientific progressive alienist (?)—a religious monomaniac!!

Just at that time the doctors believed that I needed to have the body purged to stop my folly. And they administered to me, for that effect, by big glassfuls, a medicine black and thick as syrup. True, I needed a purgation. But it was the mind that ought to be purged of that false idea. Otherwise you may clean fifty times his intestines and I tell you that will in no wise help the patient, it is certain. No, the doctors are here mistaken, blinded, surely. The trouble is not at all in the bowels. It is in the mind. The trouble is not physical. It is mental. It requires the application of a mental, moral, spiritual remedy to conquer it. That's it.

In the meantime as if this had been proved to me, I had this intimate conviction that my doctors knew nothing about my trouble. Thus I refused again to take this black medicine. And once, when the first keeper had violently poured into my mouth a great part of it, I quickly spewed out all I could. But for this, he struck me a violent blow with his heavy fist in the abdomen.

After being recovered I wrote several times to my wife that I suffered from a stomach pain, and I then believed as I do today, that this pain had no other cause than the blows received during our three last weeks of folly. And now mark, it would take so little to help us, and deliver us from our folly. Only purge our mind of the idea that this man is the Christ, and we are saved, healed. What human science could ever explain insanity, or conceive what it is, if it was not revealed by a man who had the experience of almost all the forms, degrees, and varieties of insanity, such as several kinds of frenzy, rage, furor, stupor, torpor, delirium, confusion, convulsion, dementia, down to the mildest forms of mania, melancholia and monomania, so-called? But now how take out of the patient's mind this false idea? That is the question. Well, since it is a fact, that many times we searched in our memory of God's word, to decide whether this patient was or not the Christ, if we had only had a New Testament to read therein: "For there shall arise false Christs and false prophets, and shall shew great signs and wonders, etc." Without doubt such a passage would have disabused and saved me. But behold! with the same persistence that the doctors had refused us to see our wife at the time of dire necessity, in like manner they now refused to us the Scriptures to read, the only efficacious means of saving us at present. Wherefore we may say, with a perfect assurance, based on conclusive facts, for the benefit of all those who have their kindred confined in this house, that the two things that could have relieved, healed and saved us—letting us see our wife in time, and giving us our Bible to read—have been obstinately refused to us in this hospital by the medical authority.

In the meantime we endured here a wretched life, singing and preaching, night and day, eating nothing but what is forced within us with a stomach pump, such are the troubles and sufferings which I imposed upon myself, in my folly, most of the time upon suggestion. Now tortured day and night to make me take my medicines, severely punished for my kneeling down before the false Christ, my singing, etc., violently stricken, kicked, maltreated, mocked and jeered at, vilified and insulted, striped several times with a heavy strap on the naked body, and even on the naked parts, having once a cane thrust in my mouth by the first keeper to stop our singing in the evening, and pushed with such violence on the cheek, that I thought that the flesh so stretched out would split for certain, and the cane's end get through the cheek; kicked violently even on the parts, and on the back of the neck, dropped from four feet high the head striking on the floor, strangled many times unto suffocation, beaten twice, in the evening, with his hands, in my face, while I had the handcuffs on, by a patient who is doing the attendant's work, so much and so hard that the blood ran out of my mouth on the bed sheets. Such is a part only of the treatment which I received in this hospital to heal me of my folly. But it is evident that such treatment may kill, not heal. Is it not so reader? Therefore it is towards the grave that we are going on at rapid strides, I and the doctors seeing and knowing it.

Only to let me die that way was probably too soft a death in the sight of my keepers. Cruelty has its peculiar

refinements. Listen: I was very afraid of that patient
who had uttered my name in Walloon. The attendants
knew it. and so Dr. Pember, so far that the doctor asked
me several times, what I had seen about that patient to be
so afraid of him. Now at this time, I was almost ready
to die, there were more patients than beds in our ward.
And the attendants took this very patient and put him to
sleep in my room, most probably in the room of the sole
patient of the ward who was afraid of him. During the
night that demoniac was speaking, singing and sometimes
screaming harshly. Almost every night he got up and
walked from one end of the hall to the other, for hours,
covered up with the blankets. He was urinating
every night on the floor while standing up and
sometimes defecating. His demons kept him awake almost all the night. But when he slept he snored in such
a way as to hinder any one in the room from sleeping.
Such is the dreadful companion that the keepers wilfully
gave me then to sleep with me for about one month.
I was only delivered of him, after being recovered, upon a
request I addressed to this effect to Dr. Pember, in a moment when I could catch the doctor in the ward, being
not accompanied by the attendants. Now, go ye again, ye
that have relatives or friends here repose quietly, believing
"That nothing is wanting for the welfare of your loved
ones," and that they have here a home, a residence, as it is
represented to you by the managers of this house! !
Jesuits!

Now I was sensible enough at the time to comprehend
perfectly that this life could not last long under such circumstances. I rejoiced about it. I considered that death
alone. in fact, could put an end to such sufferings, and I saw
it coming gladly. I was growing thin and feeble. One day
I caclulated that such a number of days more ought to end

my miserable career. In all my pains and sufferings, I never forgot my loved ones. Only a little while ago, it caused me great pain to have to die without seeing them again. I asked Dr. Craig (end of March 1885) that he would, under the police supervision, and at my expenses, allow me to go home to see them for a last time. Then a few days after I asked him only to permit me to write to them. All was refused to me. Then I committed them to the care of the Almighty and loving God, in whom I believed, assured he would take care of them. I was reconciled in my heart to them; guilty or not I forgave them, and completely at peace with respect to them, nothing now seems to connect me with the earth. I am ready to go to rest. It is not long ago either since we believed that we must sacrifice our life before this false Christ; and we had attempted to do it in some dark hour. But now we resolved to wait until death would come to deliver us. And the hour is coming indeed!

Three days later, I was so feeble that I could hardly raise my foot high enough to get out of my crib-bed. And the bones stuck out of my face stripped of flesh. Life quenches slowly. One thing however does not quench. It is the cruelty of my keepers, one would say: "tormentors." No, feeble, afflicted, miserable, such as I am, they all continued to strike, strangle and maltreat me just the same. Satan, who actuates them, has no mercy. —I know Satan, be sure of it. Said Mrs. E. G. White: "The heart can be very cruel when God's fear and love are removed." But however, soon, for us, their rage will be quenched. All they can do is to maltreat us unto death! After it is finished! As soon as this life is quenched, here, their power over us ceases. Death shall disarm them forever! This thought consoles me; for death in fact is coming.

I was come to this, when one forenoon of April, 1885, Dr. R. M. Wigginton, superintendent, with one of the assistants came in my room. And after a few moments the doctor superintendent, standing on my right hand, said to the assistant: "This man is in a bad condition." And the assistant said, "He is." And both of them went out without seeing if they could do any thing to help me. I saw no more of Dr. Wigginton until four days after my recovery. Here is a tacit acknowledgment by the doctors that they cannot cure or even relieve the insane. For if they could, I surely was then the very case in the hospital to experiment their healing science upon. But here we are condemned by the doctor superintendent and one of the assistants, I hearing it. In this the doctors agreed with me. I thought I was going to die, and it appears they deemed so; with this difference nevertheless, that knowing perfectly that it was willingly that I had ceased to eat, ceased to sleep, and that I was doing all those things for which I incurred those cruel punishments; just as sure as we state it here, in hearing the sentence pronounced by the doctors on my condition, I told myself that after all, I had but to stop this kind of living, not to be, if I would, a lost man. Thus it is evident that in my state of mind as it is, I know myself I have the power (God willing) to save my life or let it go. The doctors did not know it. And also could not. Human science goes not so far as that. "For what man knows the things of a man save the spirit of man which is in him." As for me, here is the delusion, the deception which leads me to death. I believe I am doing God's will in doing all those follies. They lead me to death; I see it, I feel it, I know it, and that is so certain that I calculate the days I could live yet, the nearest I can. Now we believe that we are doing God's will, because on all the principal points at least, we have consulted our false Christ and he has showed us we must do those things. And we believe in him on account of the signs and wonders he performed before us. Thus live and die the insane in hospitals, the doctors knowing not what is the trouble with them. Let human science therefore come with all her baggage of earthly knowledge, and her cortege of theories, and always we shall tell her, based on our experiences. As for us, we don't know much, but we really know one thing for certain, we know that the true cause of the trouble here is the evil spirit. "Satan is there, there." In the meantime, as the only means—the Bible—that could take out of our mind the false idea, is refused to us by the medical authority, we are going towards death at rapid strides.*

We must state here in passing, that it is a grave mistake to believe that the insane, because he is insane, is more or less insensible to blows and maltreatment, and that he runs gladly to the punishment. No, such is not the case at all, for I declare, as for me, I was doing those follies for which I was cruelly punished, but in trembling, believing I ought to do so, because urged always in some way to do them. And I was just as sensible to blows and maltreatment as a sane person is, perhaps more so. And I have seen that such generally is the case with the other patients.

Now two or three days more passed by in the same way after the sentence pronounced by the doctors on the patient's condition. Then one morning, for the last time, I asked myself once more, while strapped down in the room:

*In reflecting, after our recovery, how we had believed, in our folly, that we must put ourself to death, and then let ourself die to save others, deceived by the spirit of folly and evil, we have concluded that suicide is also the work of the one who is a murderer from the beginning. The victim puts himself to death, deceived by the evil spirit, who showed him that such is the only way to do right under the circumstances. Since the crime which killed Abel the just unto this day, be sure that Satan has a hand in all the crimes and suicides committed.

"Is that man really the Christ in fact?" And I set my-self again to examine the question, this time specially in the light of Scripture; not to spare my life; I had serious-ly renounced, but for truth's sake. Even at this last mo-ment, truth was precious to me. I loved it; and judged it was yet very important to know it. And while I was seeking to know whether this man was the Christ or not, lo! this passage of Scripture came right to my mind: "Wherefore if they shall say unto you, behold, he is in the desert; go not forth; behold he is in the secret chambers; believe it not. For as the lightning cometh out of the east, and shineth even unto the west; so shall also the coming of the Son of man be." And forthwith, at this flash of divine light, I told myself it is however true. The first coming of Christ was comparatively obscure, ig-nored; but the second coming shall be gloriously visible even as the lightning. And this man could be but a false Christ. "And my visions," said I; and I consulted them; and they proved to be deceitful visions. I was saved! ! This only one passage of Scripture, the right one, delivered me forever from my insanity, in taking away forever from my mind the false idea that this patient was the Christ. It was, we think, the morning of the 12th day of April, 1885. When Dr. Pember came to feed me. I told him: "I will take my dinner to-day." And he replied: "If you will promise me to take your dinner at noon, I will not feed you this forenoon." I promised him to do so, and the doctor went out. At noon, for the first time since over two weeks, I took voluntarily a great part of my dinner, then I took my supper, and I never missed a meal since. The next morning I assured myself that my prophet was but a false Christ indeed, and entirely delivered from this delusion, I felt, I knew that I had re-entered into posses-sion of my reason. Since then, I thought no more of dying, but only to revive and to go as soon as possible to rejoin my loved ones, as I declared a few days later to Dr. Pember.* But the doctors knew not I was cured. Four days later, Dr. Wigginton declared to my wife and boy that he considered my case incurable. And he had personally visited me that day! Thus so strange is this trouble that a patient may have lost or regained his reason for several days without the doctors who treat them knowing it.—Once, in ward 9 S. a French patient, after having been sensible enough for several weeks, had returned to his folly for four days without the doctor on duty becoming aware of the fact, though having met the patient. The first news that the doctor received of it was given him by the writer, who in speaking in French every day with that patient, perceived his relapse.—As for us we permanently recovered the day we commenced to re-take our meals. And that the doctors saw it not, and admit it not, that does not alter the fact. Now reader, you see what is insanity and its effects: how a man may get insane enough to do all kinds of follies, on account of a false idea implanted in his mind, by the evil spirit, and that to take away the false idea by the truth, by a passage of Scripture, (that the doctors refuse to the patients) and behold! he is again of sound mind and cured! "And the truth shall make you free."

At all events my cure effected in the manner related above, is a fact so evident that one day (June following) I explained in ward 10 S. to Dr. Pember how I had commenced my three last weeks of folly, and how by a passage of Scripture I had been delivered of my insanity, and at his request I quoted the passage to him. Then I said: "Doctor, had I not told you how I commenced and fin-

*In fact only a few weeks later, the eruption of my cheek resulting from the pressure exerted thereon to get me to take the opiate, being cured; the color of my face being restored; being shaved; having regained much fat already, and behaving very well under all circumstances, I was looking already no more as an insane, but as a sane and well man; thanks be to God.

ished my last folly you could never have known it?" And
the doctor responded: "How could I know it?" The doctor was right. "For what man knoweth the things of a
man save the spirit of a man which is in him?" But it is
precisely those things which he has in his mind, that generally cause the trouble, set the patient out of his senses,
disturb and derange him, and when the doctor avows he
cannot know them, he avows that he cannot cure or even
relieve the patient.*

Now restored to reason by the grace of God, we must
say, dear reader, that we have proved that, "It is a fearful
thing to fall in the hands of the living God." A few days
before our misfortunes we asked God to settle us on the
doctrine of "demons and hell." And he answered us. He
delivered us up to Satan, and he cast us in a kind of hell.
Thus he showed us that in fact, Satan and hell exist.
Friend, God is not mocked. To the eyes of this great God,
the damnable sin is the sin of unbelief. The Almighty
God, who spoke to men in olden times by his prophets,
and in these last days by his Son and Apostles, accompany-
ing their word by great wonders and miracles, wants us to
believe Him. That's it. The things I requested Him to
settle for me are plainly revealed in the Bible. I ought to have
read it and believed it. But for several years I was reading it almost no more, and yet, when I did, it was without respect or care God's word was become unfruitful for me.
It was not received with faith. Then "When fear cometh
as desolation, when distress and anguish cometh upon
me," I called upon the Lord, but He did not answer.—Yes,
He did. When I asked Him He would come and dwell
with us, He came with chastisement. When I asked Him
to lead and direct me by His good spirit, He sent the evil

*See chap. X, pp. 180 the renewing process of the mind where such seed may
grow.

spirit to lead me to do all the follies that the insane may do. It was well done! Because when the wisdom of God crieth without, saying: "How long, ye simple ones, will ye love simplicity? and the scorners delight in their scornings, and fools hate knowledge? Turn ye at my reproof, behold I will pour out my spirit unto you, I will make known my words unto you." We despised the call. Behold! our heart was attached to the goods of this world, and we would not loose our hold. And our eyes were surely blinded by the God of this world—Satan. And because the Lord had called and I would none of his reproof. "Then He also laughed at my calamity because I had hated knowledge and did not choose the fear of the Lord." Oh! woe to the man, reader friend, who refuses to listen to the voice of God's wisdom when it cries to him: "Be ye converted." And the message is now delivered to all. Now if some escape punishment, in some measure in this world, they shall not always escape. They surely one day must meet the Great Judge, Remunerator of all things. Reader, my friend, oh! escape now for your soul's life. Our God forgives abundantly for the sake of His beloved One! Knowing now how God must be feared, we invite every man to repentance, and to believe in Jesus Christ, to forsake sin and take Christ, before it is everlastingly too late! Now, for us, though once a great infidel, Jesus, the God Man, dying to save sinners, but risen and living forevermore; and Satan, the enemy of God and men, the prince of the power of darkness, are living realities. There is no more doubt in my mind about their real existence, than about my own existence.

Friend, the way of the transgressor is hard! Satan is a hard master to serve. I know it. I have seen it.

But the yoke of Christ is easy, and his burden light, and easy to bear.

And the only way to be delivered from the power of sin and Satan's terrible bondage, is to take upon us the yoke of Christ. Here and only here is salvation: In Christ Jesus. Without Christ, there is no peace, no rest, no life, no happiness! But only woe, slavery, misery, darkness and hell! Think of it! we must be eternally happy saved with God, or eternally miserable, damned with Satan and his angels! What will you choose? There is no repentance after death! And soon it wil be too late! "My spirit will not strive always with man," said God! Friend, the day is fast approaching when the sinners shall cry to the rocks and mountains to fall upon them, and hide them from the face of God and the wrath of the Lamb! Oh! don't, don't get lost! Why will you die? Why will you perish far away from Jesus, while God has provided such a way of salvation in Christ Jesus, the just dying for us the unjust? Now is the accepted time! To-day is the day of salvation! If you hear the voice of the Lord harden not your heart! We live now and to-morrow we may be dead! And die without Christ, without his salvation, that's to be lost, lost, lost! forever! Think of it! Remember, God Almighty has promised and sworn to bless and save us in Christ Jesus! Friend, I never made one cent in all my life by inviting my fellowmen to come to Christ to be saved. I do it for the love of God and the love of the souls of my fellowmen. I have served the world, Satan and self long and well. But Satan rewarded me with disease, the loss of my money, and misery! Thus Satan pays his servants! And you Ingersoll followers, let me tell you that I have been once myself an Ingersoll man. But Ingersoll, friends, did not give peace to my soul! To get peace, I had to come to Jesus! Friends, don't you know that Ingersoll followers die wretched, miserable, sinking down into hell! While the followers of Jesus live and die happy,

rejoicing in His arms?   Oh! I am now persuaded that in
the last day of judgment, Ingersoll shall be found a fool
and a liar, if he don't repent, and God shall be found just
and true.   My unconverted friend, you're a sinner, and as
such condemned in your sins by the right law of a right-
eous God!   Such is your condition, and no jeering, no
mockery, no science or sophistry can help you out.   You
need Christ to save you, and give you peace!   Ingersoll
cannot give you peace, because he has not peace himself!
He cannot give you life because he has it not.   He never
gave life to a single blade of grass!   But Jesus, the Son,
the Eternal Word, the Christ of God is the Prince of life!
He is life!   The principle of life dwelt in Him!   He may
give you life, eternal life!   The gift of God is eternal life
through Jesus Christ!   And He will give you peace!   A
peace solid, profound, durable, unalterable; a peace that
stands when soon the world shall be on fire!   That peace
I possess now in my soul!   Glory be to the Christ that
gives it!

And because He is the TRUTH, He'll make you know the
truth.   And with the truth that makes free, and peace
and life you'll get joy and happiness!   The happiness that
your soul craves for!

But you christian brethren don't you know that Roman
Catholicism made Voltaire!   And renegade Protestantism
of the United States, has made Ingersoll!   Alas! alas! perhaps, if we, christians, had been humble, loving, lovely
and charitable, instead of being proud, selfish and cold-
hearted as we are, Ingersoll, perhaps would have loved us,
and through us, our blessed Master, the Christ!   And to-
day perhaps he would be preaching Christ instead of
preaching Mammon!

Christian friends let us humble ourselves in the dust
and pray God, the Merciful God of Heaven, that He will

save Ingersoll and give him the pardon and peace that is proclaimed by His everlasting gospel through the atoning blood of the Lamb slain on Calvary ! !

Christian brethren do as you like. But as for me and mine. we shall kneel down before God, and pray for the salvation of Bob Ingersoll and Mark Barnum!

CHAPTER VI.

INSANITY AND THE DOCTORS.

To any intelligent reader, the perusal of this record of three months and twenty days of an insane, crazy enough at certain times, at least. to make all kinds of folly, demonstrates superabundantly, among some other things, the GREAT FACT, that the insane, all insane as he is, generally possesses a certain reason with which he constructs his plans, examines them, weighs them, modifies them. and tries to put them into execution when opportunities come. Only those plans being engendered by a distorted reason, and conceived in a troubled mind are often some acts of folly, often of inoffensive folly too, but sometimes they are some awful crimes. That is the truth about it. It has been a fatal, ruinous error partaken of by the doctors and lawyers, judges and jury-men, learned and ignorant, infidels and faithful to believe that the insane, because he is insane, has lost his reasoning powers and consciousness, so far that he generally can't know what he is doing. It has brought many persons of disordered intellect on the scaffold. Thus was brought up on the gallows the insane assassin of Garfield. Guiteau was insane. Yes, Guiteau declared sane by a council of fifteen doctors, superintend-

ent of insane asylums, presided over by the veteran Dr.
Gray, with his term of more than thirty years continuous
service in an insane asylum, Guiteau condemned to death
by the people, by the press, by an honest judge and
twelve jury-men, was a poor deluded one of the devil. He
had a demon! The terrible experiences we have had of
insanity, authorize me to judge so in his case.

Reader, listen: Just as soon as our miserable crime
was committed in that moment of supreme misfortune, deceived by the spirit of error and evil, we believed that we
had performed the best deed in the world, and that all
Wausau must be there to defend us if necessary. Then
after we believed during the eight days following that we
had committed a good, useful, necessary deed inspired by
the Holy Ghost.

If any one told me then I was out of my senses, I was
getting angry, because I considered myself wiser than all
the rest, a great personage, a holy man.

Now, who will fail to recognize here, all the character-
istics of Guiteau's folly. He was not insane, he said, and
when his defenders claimed he was insane, the only way
under the law to save his life, he got mad at them, he pretended to be sane, having removed the president inspired
by the Holy Ghost (thus fastening himself the rope
around his neck) he considered he was not an assassin,
but a great man who had committed a noble deed, useful
and necessary for the welfare of the country. Also, had
he the very idea that the American citizens would save
his life, while in fact they wanted to see him hang.

Now a great mark of insanity is excitement.*   And who

---

*Excitement and irritability is the best possible sign of a demon inside—
though. it is true that the devil inside renders not always people insane.
Thousands of christians on both sides of the Atlantic are ready to testify,
and do testify that they had the worst or most violent temper so long ago,
but since they were thoroughly converted or sanctified, they have continually
their temper under control, because Jesus in them keep now the devil out.
Glory be to the God of Heaven! Such is also my experience!

does not remember what an excitable spirit was Guiteau? In his moments of excitement he got so far as to insult his judges. Now how reconcile this conduct of Guiteau, with his intense desire to save his life, for all know that he greatly hurt himself thereby in the public opinion and in the mind of his judges? Only one explanation is possible—insanity. He excited, quarreled, moved by the spirit of excitement and folly. He can't help it.

Another sign of insanity is fright. Never before my attack of insanity, nor after, have I been so afraid of men, and things, and especially of death at times. I saw also that fright in my insane brother. Now, who does not know the fright of Guiteau at death at the time of the attempts made on his life in jail? Once, after the shooting at him, he prayed aloud a great part of the night. Ah! yes, Guiteau after his crime, was disgustingly afraid of death, but he couldn't help it. The devil after giving him all the boldness he needed to commit the crime, scared him almost to death after the crime. That's it.

Now all generally believed at the time of his trial, I as well as the rest, and probably many believe so to-day, that Guiteau wanted to impose upon his judges, the jury and the country, to save his life, when he contended he had committed the deed inspired by the Holy Ghost, though he was truly in earnest in his declaration. But now after the awful experiences we have had of insanity, I really believe that Guiteau was here sincere. Guiteau was a poor monomaniac laboring under the *idea* that he, himself must, to do right, remove the president Garfield for the greatest good of the country. (And is it not improbable that in doing so, he, at the same time, satisfied some secret desire of revenge.) But at any rate so deluded, that he really believed that the inspiration, the pressure came from the Holy Ghost, while in fact it was suggested by the evil spirit. I know what it is to be troubled with monomania, so-called. I once really believed that I, myself, must die to save the rest of the sinners; and under this delusion I renounced the desire to live, and let myself nearly die, after some real attempt at suicide.

In conclusion, now over three years after my recovery, I always believe, both, the one and the other, that we have been *inspired* to commit our bloody deed; only we have been inspired, not by the Spirit of God, which is a spirit of order, peace, love and mercy, but by the spirit of the one who is a murderer from the beginning. We have been inspired, possessed (although of course in some different degree) by the spirit of error and evil and folly. And being so inspired, possessed, is to be demoniac, is to be insane. That's the state of mind of all the unfortunates who fill our insane hospitals. Therefore we conclude that Guiteau mounted the scaffold insane. His demeanor on the scaffold, singing with the rope around his neck, etc., confirms our conclusion; as also the fact that Guiteau at the moment of being launched into eternity, to appear before the Most High Judge—in whom he firmly believed —he persisted yet in his declaration that he had removed the president inspired by the Holy Ghost. Therefore to render a right sentence in the nature of the case, jury and judges ought to condemn the devil to be hung, if possible, who had certainly inspired the deed, and send Guiteau into an insane asylum. But alas! here judges and jurymen could hardly help it. They acted according to the decision of the doctors who pronounced Guiteau sane. Therefore let us see about those ones.

In fact, is it not pitiable to hear Dr. Superintendent Gray, with his blind science, make an argument in favor of Guiteau's sanity because he pretended himself to be sane. Ah ! *docte* science, don't you know that the characteristic of the insane is to consider himself to be wise alone, and all the rest fools, and very often considers himself to be a great personage? * All this we said, was the characteristic of the insane Guiteau.

And is it less edifying to hear Dr. Gray, who presided over this council of Grecian Wises who sent Guiteau to the gallows, declare before the world that insanity is a disease of the brain, of the body, and because he had found no bodily disease in the examination he had of Guiteau's life, concluding that he was of sound mind ? Ah ! *docte* science, don't you know now after thirty years personal practice in insanity that a person with a sound brain and sound body may be insane and do all kinds of follies, and that all it requires to deliver him of his folly is to cast out the demon who renders him insane ? Now, having been myself one of the most insane, with the most sound body —and brain probably—and in view of the observations we have made on the insane while we have lived, eaten, drank, worked, played and slept with them, we conclude that Guiteau, though apparently in good physical health, had nevertheless the mind deranged. In the meantime if the doctor continue to pretend that Guiteau was sane, let him show that there may exist beside Guiteau, another sane man able and willing to assassinate a president and a great citizen to advertise the book he proposes himself to publish. If such conception has been engendered in a sane mind let the doctor show us what else insanity is !

But again Dr. Gray tells us: "And the presence in him (in Guiteau) of reason, judgment, reflection and self-control in regard to his act, controls me in forming my opinion."(The opinion that Guiteau was sane.) Old senseless

*Of course we don't mean that all the insane are such. Some in the asylums know they are insane and deplore it at times. Some persons outside more or less deranged, and aware of their trouble, conceal it more or less, and even some may themselves consult the doctors about their trouble.

doctor ! Why not then open the doors of the hospitals to all those patients who possess reason, judgment, reflection and self control to construct their plans, and wait for the favorable moment to put them into execution, and leave only the blind and paralytics therein ? for scarce indeed are the patients who have not their plans and reason thereupon. And why not proclaim of sound mind the woman who waited for the moment when her husband had left the house, to assassinate all her children by the ways and means she had chosen after some plans well concocted, and then suicided herself ?

No, but it appears here clear to all that with some conclusions a great deal less arbitrary than the ones of Dr. Gray in regard to Guiteau's sanity we could conclude that the veteran doctor who boasts to have never pronounced sane an insane or insane a sane person, would be a subject a good deal more fit for a patient in an insane asylum than to be superintendent of the same. *

Now, while the doctors—and they are many, and great, and learned—proclaim unanimously by their science that insanity is a disease of the brain, we, poor, alone and ignorant, based on our experiences and on the everlasting word of God, we say, no, insanity is not a disease of the brain; it is a trouble of the mind. It is not a disease of the physical man, but a trouble of the mental, moral man. And here we assume this position, that a person may be insane enough to make all kind of follies, and be in possession of a sound brain and sound body. Now why do the doctors proclaim that insanity is a disease of the brain against the declarations of God's word, and against the positive facts revealed by the positive science of anatomy, which demonstrate that the immense majority of the dissected brains of

---

*A few weeks after the above was written for the first time, we learned with regret, of the death of Dr. Gray, through the press.

the insane are in no wise different from the brains of sane persons ? Well, the Catholic priest seeing he could make no profit of the scriptural doctrine of "Paradise and Hell" invented his purgatory and he derived a great profit therefrom. In like manner the doctor who could make no profit of the rational and scriptural doctrine that insanity is a trouble of the mind—*a demoniacal possession*—has proclaimed that insanity is a "B-r-a-i-n d-i-s-e-a-s-e" consequently physical, treatable and curable by medical science. And some of them realize also fair benefit therefrom ! But alas ! alas ! What about our brethren, the insane, delivered up into their hands !

We must not of course, overlook the positive influence of the mind on the body, and vice versa. Thus, for instance, let a man of sound mind indulge in too large libations of strong drink, and he may more or less lose his mind and reason. A starving person gets often delirious. Fever brings delirium. A drowning person lost his mind in the waters. Most probably also a person dying by strangulation. A person may get insane from head injury and insolation. From the evil effects of intemperance, masturbation and through some other disease. Probably almost any physical disease, if intensified enough, may lead to insanity.* We also believe in the hereditary predisposition to insanity. But all this does not hinder insanity from being pre-eminently a trouble of the mind, and also that when a person is insane, no matter what

*On the other hand a person not nervous may become very nervous if he gets insane. Also the red rose color of a person's face changes very often to a grayish disagreeable color when getting insane. We found in some insane rigidity or relaxation of the muscles. And often the results of a poor blood circulation, manifested by giving a blue color to the skin of the hands and nails, and keeping them cold. And some other alterations of the body, in its appearance and functions, may take place as results of insanity. "Man," said rightly Capt. K. Carter, in his 'Divine Healing,' "has a dual nature, and each half is itself a duality." In fact, man is composed of body and soul. The soul comprises our spiritual and moral nature. The body the physical and mental nature. Now this division of our being rather comprises, we think, the four principal ways or channels through which a person may actually get insane.

may be the cause ascribed for it, the result is the same in all cases, that is, to be insane is to be demoniac, and Satan is the spirit who works in every insane with more or less power and manifestation, as we have demonstrated.

But now where is the seat and seed of insanity? Insanity, or mental alienation has its seat and germs in the human heart. Sin springs from the heart, and sin is itself an immense folly—insanity in some sense. The commands of God are right and holy. Their observance produces peace, purity, and happiness. Sin is the transgression of the law, and it produces trouble, impurity and misery. The desperately wicked human heart by its natural rebellion against God's law, contains in itself folly, insanity in germs. In fact it is folly to swear, curse, and blaspheme against God. It is folly to lie, steal, to commit adultery, to hate, maltreat and kill his neighbor. It is folly to be proud, selfish. jealous. impure and lazy, and to get drunk and angry. But now all those follies, germs of insanity exist in the human heart.* And how does insanity come forth? Well let us try a little comparison. Certain it is that generally every woman bears in the ovaries the germs of a family. But it needs the action of the male to fecund those germs. And from the natural union of man and woman there comes forth children. Now, all those germs of insanity in the human heart need also the action of some one to fecund them. That one exists. It is the devil. Satan has the power to enter into the human heart and possess it. Christ says so. And from this infernal, but possible union of Satan with the human heart, there comes forth a child. Its name is, INSANITY. Here is the fatherhood and motherhood of insanity. The devil and the human heart. Now let us follow the CHILD in its mad career, words and deeds, and we

*Read Mark VII, 21, 22, 23.

will find that generally the characteristic of the insane, whether it bears the name of maniac, melancholiac, dement, paretic, monomaniac, etc., is pride, great pride, egotism, anger, excitement, impurity, wickedness, murder. But all those things are of the devil, and are contained in germs in the human heart. And their undisguised manifestation or explosion, under the power of the devil, constitutes insanity. That's what insanity is. Therefore Satan and the human heart are the legitimate parents of insanity. Yes, and their abode is hell. Yes, and if any person would experience in this world some of the anguish and horrors of hell, it suffices for him to get insane. Hell exists. It is a real abode.

But now, what about the doctors who extract the healthy ovaries by the dozen from the insane women, under pretext of removing their insanity! Oh! senseless medical science, how cruel art thou! Thou hast mutilated the living, and cut in pieces all the brains of the dead insane thou couldst get in possession of, and some of their spinal cords too, to seek insanity in the body, while it is not in the body, but in the mind, in the heart, in the soul. Doctor, insanity is in thy own heart and mind, ready to spring forth at any given moment, under the power of the evil one. Cease then to torture and mutilate the flesh to seek to cure a trouble which is in the mind and sentiment.

Oh senseless medical science! how many sufferings and tortures thou hast uselessly inflicted on our unfortunate brethren and sisters, fallen into thy hands! Oh! who shall deliver our loved ones from thy grasp! Now, brethren citizens, when this senseless medical science has gone so far in its ruinous, fatal blindness as to extract the healthy ovaries of insane women by the dozen in the sole city of New York to remove their insanity, if in presence of such treatment, and of all the rough, cruel, violent, senseless

and inhuman treatment administered to the insane, if you
don't find that it is high time now to take our insane out of
its hands to treat them ourselves according to common sense
and reason and the Scriptures, then if the doctors kill your
insane again, beware that God does not require some day
their blood from you who have mercilessly delivered up
those unfortunates into the hands of this blind and senseless medical science.

Among some others, a palpable proof of the utter ignorance of the doctors about insanity, is the very fact of
all their contradictions.   They have written books after
books, the ones to contradict or try to destroy what the others
had previously said; and of all that literature no practical
good has resulted towards curing the insane, for the insane
rather recover while in care of people who ignore the contents of those books, as at Gheel, etc.   One doctor defines
insanity to be this, another to be that, and no one has
found what is the true cause of the trouble.   Some say
that the cause of insanity is in the brain, some in the
spinal cord, some say it is in the blood, some others in the
bowels, and some believe it is in the genital apparatus, or
ovaries.*   Thus some doctors remove the ovaries of insane women; some purge the bowels of their patients,
some bleed them, yes, and some administer the insane
phosphorus, calomel, opium, morphia, strychnia, hyosciamia, alcohol, paraldehyde, electricity, etc., generally not
knowing themselves why or how such remedy could help
the patients.   And while the doctors have thus tried
remedies after remedies, drugs after drugs, means after
means, of course the insane die in their hands, in their

*Since any particle of the human body is susceptible of disease, of course
we don't mean at all that some insane may not suffer of one or several of
those or other ailments. But the great fact is that the insane has the mind,
reason, feelings affected and the trouble most generally demands a moral
treatment. Hence the inability of the M. D.s, to cure insanity by medical
appliances.

folly, while they rather recover without doctors or medicines kept at home, at Gheel. or in certain hospital receptacles such as those of New Zealand.*   For us, such
is our testimony: While insane. ready to die in the hands
of the three doctors of the Northern Wisconsin Hospital;
condemned by them, the Lord Jesus Christ renders me to
reason by a passage of His word divine.   Glory be to His
great name forever!

In the meantime the doctors have thrown dust in the
eyes of the people. in reporting the several recoveries of the
same patient. as so many patients recovered. so that, for
instance, a patient who had been discharged as recovered
10, 15, 20 or 30 times, after so many attacks, figured in
their reports as 10, 15, 20 or 30 patients recovered, while
in reality such patient being possibly again re-admitted for
a subsequent attack, no one patient had recovered.

And while our insane hospitals multiplied and yet are
overflowing, and the overflowing population sent from
time to time in county asylums, the doctors alienists boast
of their scientific progress in insanity, and say they may
cure 60, 70, 80 or more per cent. of the most common
forms of insanity "under proper treatment."

What proper treatment!   By what kind of treatment
can they cast out the devil?   What is the matter after
all with those doctors?   Are they blind, or knave, or both?
The truth is that the doctors ignoring completely the true
cause of insanity—Satan—they generally speak of the
trouble as the blind speak of colors, and are powerless to
cure or even relieve the patients.

*Read "The Curability of Insanity" by Dr. P. Earle.

+Read the same book. Now the reader who might read Dr. Pliny Earle's
book will notice that when he speaks of the deceiving reports of the doctors,
of the powerlessness of their remedies to cure insanity, of the inability of
the doctor alienists to rightly judge of a person's state of mind, that in all
this, sustained by facts, he is strong as a tower. But as soon as he attempts
to defend the insane asylums as curative institutions, he puts Dr. Earle in
contradiction with his own declarations or quotations.

Let us now hope that the most honest among them, will themselves loudly proclaim it as they will get aware of the fact. God, honesty and humanity require it. For it is evident that the greatest woe for the insane, arises from the failure of the doctors to proclaim their powerlessness to cure insanity and epilepsy.

But to return to my adventures. Having learned I was almost dying in the hospital, my wife requested once more from the doctor superintendent to see me. And the doctor having at last permitted her, she came for the first time, with our boy, the 16th day of April, 1885, as stated. Why and how does the doctor superintendent permit her to see me this day, when the imperious necessity for me to see her exists no more, whereas he has refused such permission for three months, and when her visit would probably have saved me from the woes of my three last weeks of boisterous folly, which have led me almost into the grave? Let Dr. Wigginton explain this! And suffice it for us to say that that visit of my wife after all my pains, anguish, and sufferings did me great good nevertheless. And great also was the poor little thing's surprise to find in me a quiet man clothed, sitting and in his right mind, who spoke with her during three days and telling her nothing but what was sensible and reasonable. For the doctor superintendent in his letter of the previous day, had but told her of my irrational talk and delusions, save he said, that I had commenced to eat again. But the truth is that the very day I started to r take my meals, is the day I had been delivered from my folly. It is so evident that the doctor superintendent had even no idea that I had recovered, that he then told my wife and boy, that as for him, he regarded my case as incurable. Then five months afterwards (August following) he wrote her again: "He is not cured and may break down at any time."

But since the time of my wife's first visit, she, from the letters I wrote her regularly every week, and I upon what I felt and knew by experience about insanity, both of us have judged always, that God had permanently cured me, and knew it and saw it. Whence it appears that a person without learning may judge better of the state of mind of some one with whom he is in continual contact than some doctor superintendents with their lame science may do. Why not? Whereas Satan renders the patient insane, the doctors can, no better than you and I, cope with the devil. That's it.

Now it would surely be edifying for the public if our space would permit it, to relate the history of the treatment of a certain headache of ours by the hospital's doctors, to relate how for ten long weary months they have obliged the patient to take for that headache a worthless medicine, intended to purify the blood in spite of all the protestations of the patient addressed to Dr. Pember to get him to stop the medicine, and after a fair trial of six months of it without any relief whatever therefrom, the patient established before Dr. Pember, in a very clear and substantial manner, we believe, that the cause of the headache was not the impurity of the blood, but the congestion of the blood. No doubt it would be edifying to hear how Dr. Pember accused and condemned Dr. Craig, his colleague, for having changed the medicine, and how Dr. Craig condemned this saying of Dr. Pember in telling repeatedly that he had not changed the medicine, but had only added a tonic to it because, taken pure, it weakens the patient; and to hear how in the forenoon of the 22nd of March, 1886, between 9 and 10 o'clock, Dr. Craig passed pure and simple condemnation on this treatment of our headache by his colleague Dr. Pember, for the last past eight months; and how in spite of this and of the reiterated protestations of the patient, the same medicine was continued. And without doubt it would be edifying to explain that the patient, in the fourteen months he has been detained in the hospital after his recovery, told time and again to Dr. Wigginton he had headache, that the doctor superintendent never, never addressed the least question to the patient to try to discover the cause of it, and that he nevertheless ordered that the same medicine be continued, so said Dr. Pember. And that worthless medicine was administered to us three times daily until the last day we staid in the hospital to stop my headache which continued all that time. Also Dr. Pember advised me to use it after being out of the hospital. But the very day I was liberated I ceased to take all medicine and soon I got better. Of course the headache comes sometimes again, but now liberated for almost two years we have generally felt better since leaving the hospital without doctor or medicine. (Glory be to God!) Whence it necessarily results, that that treatment of the headache by the doctors of the Northern Wisconsin Hospital, was just sheer charlatanism, as I had suspected it to be for long months before leaving, and declared it to Dr. Pember.

Now let the good people of Wisconsin consider, if the doctors of this hospital thus dose and drug a patient able to speak, protest and reason with them, how awfully they might dose and drug our unfortunate insane more or less bereaved of reason.

Citizens, as for me, I am neither doctor nor druggist, I am nothing but a simple workingman, and also a great sinner saved by grace; therefore it is not I who condemn the doctors of that hospital, but you hear it, it is the doctors themselves who have taken charge to condemn themselves. Dr. Pember condemns Dr. Craig. And Dr. Craig condemns Dr. Pember and his treatment, and in condemning each one separately, they condemn both of them mutually and conjointly, whereas both of them have participated in the same treatment, both of them acknowledging it. Of course I wish no harm to those doctors. God bless them and save them! But what about our poor brethren fallen into such medical hands!!

I had caught in the hospital an ugly eruption on my legs, which the doctors could not cure. One evening in December, 1885, I spoke of it, for the second time to the doctor Supt., and I asked him if he knew of any thing to heal it. The doctor Supt. told me, no, and that the eruption was the result of my nervousness. But to prove that the eruption was in no wise the result of a nervous state, just from that time the eruption healed permanently as Dr. Pember ascertained it. It was just an evening of dancing. Dr. Wigginton exerted on me the most diabolical pressure, to oblige me to go to dance against my feelings and the most express dictate of my heart and conscience. He and Dr. Craig have exercised the same pressure on some other patients, to get them to dance against their feelings and conscience. As we know some have given up and go to the dance. And two have resisted. But to thus morally torture intelligent patients to get them to a dance, or some other party against their feelings, and express dictates of their conscience, should surely be speedily stopped.

The spring following, having resolved to buy some books to read in the hospital, my wife in coming to visit me had left me the necessary money to buy them, which money I innocently deposited in the hospital's office. But when I asked Dr. Pember to send the price of those books with the orders, he answered me that I had a wife in Wausau to buy me some books if I needed some. Besides that I could speak of it to the Dr. Supt. Then the first time I saw Dr. Wigginton, I presented my request. And he asked me, "What are the books you want to buy?"

"Here they are," said I, and I gave the doctor a written list:

1. The Fall of the Great Republic.
2. The United States in the Light of Prophecy.
3. Plain Home Talk. (Medical work)
4. Treatise on Insanity.

The doctor superintendent read the list, then told me that the reading of those books was not good for me. I asked him four times to send the price of those books from my money, and every time he refused to do it, because all those books written by *cranks*, he said, were not good reading for me. At the time I had regained my reason for over ten months, I had read and written very much during that time, almost continually, and thereby knowing better than any doctor the effects that such reading could produce on my mind, and at the same time knowing the real value of such declarations of the hospital's doctors, and to a great extent their knowledge about insanity, I therefore wrote orders for three of those books, and sent them to my wife, who forwarded them to their addresses with the price of the books. When she had received them, she sent me those books to the hospital. And after I had read a good part of them, the three hospital doctors declared one after the other that I looked well, very well. And a little while later I was liberated. Surely the world has never been lacking in charlatans! What the people must specially know, is, that the treatment of the insane here, is sheer charlatanism. But now if the doctor superintendent believed as he asserted, that the reading of those books was going to hurt my mind, behold! how he is misled by his blind science! And if he does not believe it, what show of ill-disposition towards the patient!

Now we have seen how it was refused to me to see my wife in time of dire necessity, and how when in so great need of it, the Bible was refused to us. The Bible has been in like manner refused to some other patients. And I have heard Dr. Wigginton advise the reading of novels instead to some patient deeply religious.

Now, this man Dr. Wigginton, who judged of the state of mind and nervousness of the patients, as we see he judged in our case, who refuses to them the things which could cure and save the patients, and prescribes for them useless medicines, novels, dances, spectacles, card and checker plays, and the use of the swab, sand bag and strap, has been for three long years (from 1884 to 1887) superintendent of the Northern Wisconsin Hospital.* After his forced resignation (1887) the board of supervision thought they could not do better than to re-appoint in that charge, Dr. Walter Kempster, who had been for twelve years superintendent of the same hospital.

But four months after his second appointment Dr. Kempster resigned and was replaced (January 1888) by Dr. C. E. Booth.

Now before putting this work under press, the 24th of May, 1888, I left Minneapolis for Oshkosh, and the next day, the 25th, about 10 o'clock a. m. I entered the Northern Hospital again; this time to visit the wards.

That some nice looking reporters, elegantly dressed, the head covered with a shining silk stove-pipe, and the whole—head and hat of course—supported by a nice

---

*Of course great noise has been made last summer (1887) about the inability and incompetency of Dr. R. M. Wigginton. But now in supposing, as the Wisconsin newspaper men affirm that Dr. W. Kempster and even Dr. C. E. Booth possess some psychological knowledge that the rather eccentric alienist Dr. Wigginton lacks, yet while Satan is the true cause of insanity and epilepsy, Drs. Kempster or Booth can no better cope with the devil nor cast him out of the insane than Dr. Wigginton. Hence it would be the sheerest folly to expect more recoveries on account of those late changes in the superintendency of the Northern Wisconsin Hospital.

white stiff collar about a half a foot high, wearing large, stiff, inconvenient cuffs, ornamented with a pair of golden buttons; and wearing a shining golden watch chain that would hold a good sized dog; that such gentlemen are readily and amicably received to investigate the wards, by the doctor Supt., I readily believe. But as the writer has not the means nor inclination to wear such apparel, it cost him patient efforts, courage and persistence to be admitted to see all the wards. Listen: In entering the hospital I told the old door keeper to go and tell the doctors I wanted to visit the wards. He told me that every afternoon at two o'clock some one conducted the visitors through the wards; that I could come at that time. "Go and tell the doctors I wish to see part of the wards this forenoon and the rest in the afternoon," said I. He went and came back with the answer that the doctor Supt. was not there, and that it needs a special order from him to visit the wards in the forenoon. I told him to inform the doctor Supt. as soon as he came to his office, that I wished to visit part of the wards in the forenoon. He did so. When the Dr. Supt. repaired, not very anxious to meet the humble but importunate visitor! he walked a little around the front of the hospital, then he appeared in the waiting room door, and asked me what I wanted. "To visit the wards," I said, "I'll send you some one to show you them," he responded and disappeared. A few minutes after appeared the supervisor Roberts, with his embarassed air, and his well known face reflecting a troubled conscience, and he said, "We will wait to see if others come upon the train." Another man entered and Roberts proceeded towards the wards. And I told him I wanted to visit all the wards. "We don't show all the wards but only some of them" he responded. He conducted us through a few wards of male and female patients, he showed us the dancing hall, then he re-entered the long corridor and said, "That's all I can show you." "I'll see the doctor Supt.," said I. A few minutes later, seeing Dr. Booth at hand, I went straight to him and told him, "The supervisor has showed me a few wards, but I wish to see all of them." And he said, "We will go and see them," and came along right away. It was then after 11 o'clock. And from this moment until I left him, definitely at 8 p. m., Dr. Booth, who had been perhaps, a little stiff-necked first, was with me right along with exemplary complacency. He readily granted all my requests regarding investigation, answered diligently and benevolently all my questions, hearkened attentively to any suggestion of ours, opened every door at my request and told the employes to do so. While we passed through some of the men wards strenuous efforts were made by some attendants to make the doctor Supt. know I had previously been in the hospital. I prevented it by a severe constant watching. In wards Nos. 5 and 6 an old *madre* attendant, who could stand it no longer, broke out and said aloud, "Mr. D—— you know how things run in this ward." And he spoke some other things pertaining to my ancient dealings in regard to some old patients with the same purpose. Dr. Booth did not understand what the smart man meant, I think, and he only learned that I had been in the hospital when I told him myself in ward 9 S., and in due time.

Now so far as we can judge we have found Dr. C. E. Booth, a gentleman with more or less good intentions and dispositions, in view of the most singular position he occupies; that is, having to treat patients, the true cause of whose trouble he completely ignores. And right here, we must call the attention of the people to the GREAT FACT that the evil in this institution—in these institutions—is so deep, so profound, of so long standing, and of such nature that it CANNOT be removed by the mere change of superintendency.

Listen: When I and the other demented patients were here beaten, kicked, strangled, dropped, abused, maltreated, mocked, vilified, with no necessity whatever, it was under Dr. R. M. Wigginton, who bears the name too of a good disciplinarian. Now some of the attendants who maltreated and abused the patients that way had been employed under Dr. Walter Kempster's first administration. They have stayed in the service of the hospital during Dr. R. M. Wigginton's administration (1884-'87). They have been still employed during Dr. Kempster's second administration of four months (August, 1887, to December). And now those same attendants and the same nightwatch and the same cruel patient helping the attendants in ward 5 and 6 whom WE HAVE SEEN treat the patients as WILD BEASTS ARE THERE STILL under Dr. Charles E. Booth's administration. Would it not be then the sheerest folly on the part of the people to believe that the patients are now humanly treated, when Dr. Booth, superintendent incumbent, employs the very same rough, cruel, violent, senseless, inhuman employes?

In fact we have found patients sleeping in crib-beds and some locked up in bedrooms at noon since morning, with no justifying reason whatever. We have found some poor, quiet paralytic in the wards of the howling, violent maniacs.* We have found patients of good sense, who would probably make good, useful, working, producing citizens at large, detained in the hospital, at the expenses of the tax payers, and against their deep, earnest desires

---

*We have also found the case of a young idiot girl whose parents must be just as idiotic in some respect as their infant, to send her in the hospital, to be therein eventually very much maltreated instead of taking good care of the poor little dear innocent one at home.

to be set free. And we have ascertained in presence of Dr. Superintendent Booth, that the employes do now—as they have done for years and years—eat butter, cakes, pies, good pieces of meat, and drink milk and coffee, while our unfortunate brethren the patients are wrongly deprived of those things.

Of course no patient was strangled that day in our presence, but while those who strangled them are still employed, would it be reasonable to believe they strangle them now no more? As for us, suffice to say that we have the assurance that the patients are still here abused, maltreated. No argument can destroy this fact.

Dr. Booth showed me Siebling's room, and after supper spoke at length of this case, and told me the motives and feelings with which he permitted the removal of the patient who died on his way home. My impression about this case is just this: That it is possible that Dr. Booth might have permitted the removal of the patient, intending to do right, in behalf of both the sick man and wife. But that the patient Siebling had been abused, maltreated in the hospital, it could hardly be otherwise while he was in the violent ward where I have seen all the demented patients, as a general rule, beaten, kicked, strangled, etc.. and also patients more or less quiet for the slightest offence, or no offence at all. I really believe that this decision of ours, in the present case, will stand in the day of the searching judgment to come.

But now in passing, what about those reporters who after a long investigation in this hospital reported to their respective papers that all is for the best in this house? Ah! *Messieurs!* let me tell you that in doing so you, yes, you, yourself are helping, consciously or unconsciously those who abuse our unfortunate brethren and sisters here! And then Messieurs! if you do such criminal work for the sake of money, ah! beware! beware! for the God of Heaven who hates to thus see treated the widow, the orphan and the afflicted watches over you!! And if you are not acquainted Messieurs! with the secrets of the running of such institutions, then let them alone. Don't, don't at least deceive the people about the treatment of their loved ones locked up in this house of woe and torture! for God and humanity's sake!

The employes of this hospital seem not to have the least idea that they ought to be the servants of the patients and of the people. On the contrary they sneered and mocked at the citizen visitors who pay and feed them with their own money, in the most silly way, when they get a chance. Of this I had the honor to inform Dr. Superintendent Booth, who admitted the fact by a timely and respectful silence. This in regard specially to the female employes. And I learned that, in the evening around the depot, the males were barking and raging at me, because having surprised them in their iniquities and greediness. I had severely reproved them in presence of the doctor superintendent in behalf, of course, of our wronged, maltreated, abused brethren, the insane.

What it needs here, is a thorough and honest investigation of the affairs of this house, to reveal to the people the enormity of the iniquity of this infamous house!

Let us have it!

The 7th of June, 1888, at half past 9 o'clock a. m. we entered the insane asylum at St. Peter, Minnesota, and informed the doctors that I wished to visit all the wards. I was introduced to Dr. Arthur F. Kilbourne, second assistant physician. After having asked him a few questions pertaining to the running of the institution, Dr. Kilbourne wanted to know if I was collecting those particulars for the press and what paper I represented. I told him in all truth, "I represented nobody but myself." He then introduced me to Dr. John H. James, first assistant physician, acting now as superintendent, in the absence of Dr. Cyrus K. Bartlett. superintendent, being in Europe at present. After a few questions from both parties, Dr. James asked me in virtue of what authority I was there to investigate. I answered, "Dr. this is a state institution, and as such it must be opened for investigation to any citizen. That's my only right." He admitted the fact and said he would send me some one to conduct me through the wards, and charged the first supervisor to do it. The supervisor came and he opened the wards. When Dr. James passed by, he stayed a little while with me. Then excusing himself, he set another employe to conduct me. Then Dr. Kilbourne came along and stayed with me visiting the wards until noon. At noon he repaired to the corridor of the main building, and after having agreed with me that I should see the rest of the wards after dinner, he took me to Dr. James' office. After some new inquiries about my object of investigation. and for what paper it was, I then told Dr. James I wished to be conducted through a few wards while the patients were taking their dinner. He objected to that, first, because no employe was then at hand to conduct me. I readily set aside that futile objection. But then he said that the presence of a visitor would annoy the patients while eating and prevent them from taking a good meal, and thus objected to my being in the wards "in behalf of his patients." "Doctor," said I, "I have lived with the insane, I have eaten, drank, worked and slept with them: I know very well their feelings. Now I tell you I will not annoy or hurt them, or even speak to them while eating. I only desire to pass through a few wards while they take their dinner; have you well understood the nature of my request?" He says, "Yes, I have."

But nevertheless he objected. After he had several times refused to let me be among them while eating, he repeated that he did so "in behalf of his patients." Then we fixed the time to visit the rest of the wards after dinner. And I said to him, "Sir, I go to the waiting room and will wait there until you'll be ready for business." And I quietly repaired to the waiting room. But only a few minutes after Dr. James entered, and told me (in violation of his previous word and of Dr. Kilbourne's) "We have no secret, but I object to any further investigation of yours without an order of some one of the trustees."*

But we know enough. The secret of the business is that the patients in St. Peter hospital are beaten, kicked, strangled, stricken unto blood without necessity. and they are poorly fed while the employes are well fed. and the doctors keep these things hidden in the darkness so far as they can. Now we know that these things are so beyond contradiction, and that an honest, well conducted investigation will reveal to the people of Minnesota cases of abuse and maltreatment worse than this. Whether the doctors admit it or deny it makes no difference: the facts are such and no argument, no science or sophistry can ever destroy those sad, but REAL, LIVING, EXISTING FACTS.

We believe we have done our duty in telling those things to the people of Minnesota themselves to see if they want to stop or let continue such an awful, disastrous state of things in their insane hospitals.

After having asked and received from Dr. James the last biennial report of the Minnesota hospitals for insane, I then repaired to St. Peter city, took the 11:10 p. m.

---

*Those doctors have always said too much or not enough. Then they take back their word or add to it to make it of more effect. No wonder about it. How could they speak right while they are not right in their heart and conscience? The truth is that some deeds of darkness are committed here and they hate the light. Children of darkness, they try to hinder their deeds from being brought to light.

Northwestern train for Rochester. And the 8th of June at 9 o'clock we presented ourself to the Second Hospital for Insane at Rochester. I told the usher I wished to visit the hospital and told him to inform the doctors of it. He went to the doctors' office and told them so. and sometime after he came himself to conduct me through the wards. Before entering the first ward I told him I wanted to see all the wards. And he told me they didn't show all the wards to visitors. but only a few of them. He conducted me through four of the men wards, then went to the main corridor and told me that was all he could show me. I told him, "Please go and tell the doctors I wish to see every ward, and I will wait for your answer in the waiting room." I went there and waited patiently for some time. Then a middle sized gentleman entered, announced himself as Dr. Phelps, second assistant, and asked me what I wanted. I told him that the usher had showed me a few wards. but I wished to see all the wards. male and female. He told me I could not see them. Then he asked me what right I had to ask to see all the wards. "Sir" said I, "this is a state institution, sustained, maintained by the people's money, and it ought to be open to any visitor." That's all. I asked him if he was acting by order of the doctor superintendent. He said, "he was." Then I told him, "Sir, I wish to see all the wards, such is my request. It belongs now to you to grant it or refuse it. What do you say?" But he went away without giving any answer, appearing to be called away for some other business. I waited a little while. No answer. I went and took a drink in the drug store, and seeing Dr. Phelps on the porch uselessly assisting some ladies in a hack, when he got through, I asked him if he wanted to refuse or grant my request. He demanded a little more time to see about it. And after having probably talked the matter over with the other doctors, he sent the druggist to conduct me through the rest of the men wards. And we went. But in the meantime, the patients being about all out, there was nothing to see but empty wards, (just what the managers wanted,) except we met a few patients here and there stopped in the wards; some of them being left there in violation of the order of Dr. Superintendent Bowers to take such patients out, and we met a few of them in bed. Since there was almost nothing to see at the time, in the men wards, I asked the druggist, my conductor, to go and spend that time in some of the women wards. He said there was only a few more of the male wards to see; he conducted me through those empty wards, then went back to the main corridor. Here Dr Phelps met us. He opened one of the women wards and conducted me in the first part of it. And while I was to proceed further, he abruptly cut off my visit, and led me out He came along in the library, where I had my *hardes*, and I asked him when he would be ready to show me the rest. "What rest," said the doctor. "The women wards, sir, I have only visited the men wards." I responded. And he said he thought I had seen enough, that they had been with me for two hours already, and that no man had ever made such request.* "Sir," said I, "I wish to be conducted now into a few of the men wards while they are taking their dinner. Not to trouble or annoy the patients while eating or even speak to them, I only desire to pass through some of the wards; and then to see all the female wards in the afternoon. Such is my request. It belongs to you to grant it

---

*Dr. James of St Peter asylum objected to my being conducted into all the wards on the ground that if they do that with the visitors they could not do the rest of their work. But the truth is, as stated by Dr. Phelps here, that never a visitor requested to see all the wards, and that the real hidden motive not to show me them all was the fear that I might discover something wrong. That's all.

or refuse it. As for me I believe I have done my duty in
making it." Dr. Phelps then asked me what I wanted to
do with those particulars I sought for. "I am not obliged
to tell you what I want to do, but I am just preparing a
little work on insanity and insane asylums, and I wished
to visit all the wards of this hospital to tell in that publication what I shall deem proper about it." said I. Dr. Phelps
asked me: "Are you a doctor?" "I am not, sir, I have
never studied medicine." "Then you have no business to
write about that," he said. "Sir," said I, "I know what I
speak about. Then the people will judge as to
whether I speak good or bad." Dr. Phelps contented
himself with this, and contested no more my right
to write about insanity, but he nevertheless repeatedly refused to let me see anything else about the hospital. But thanks be to God, Drs. Phelps, nor Collins, 1st
assistant, nor Bowers, superintendent, could hinder us
to learn that the patients are abused, thrown down on the
floor, beaten, strangled and wretchedly treated without
any necessity whatever in Rochester Insane asylum. In
both Rochester and St. Peter hospitals, there are some
patients with black eyes. When questioned about it doctors and employes pretended they get thus hurt by some
violent patients. Now we confidently believe that an
honest investigation shall establish that the patients got
those black eyes from their keepers.

But now those doctors of the Minnesota insane hospitals, more especially those at Rochester seem completely
to ignore that they run an institution of the people, built
and maintained by the people's money, and that as such
they must be opened to any visitor or investigator; and
they act here as if they manage a private institution, built
and sustained by their own money.

Dr. Booth, superintendent of the Northern Wisconsin

Hospital does not think so. On the contrary, Dr. Booth declares that "the Northern Hospital is a state institution open to any investigator," and better still, he practiced what he says in the full acceptation of the words. He accompanies the investigator, opens every ward, every room, every door at all risk. If fault is found he don't deny it, but rather apologizes. He listens to any remark or suggestions of the investigator, ready, as he said to me to abandon what he thought right yesterday or to-day, if he finds it wrong to-morrow. Well, we know that the system—now in vogue—to try to cure insanity or relieve the insane by medicine and by nearly all the other medical appliances, and to try to quiet and bring to submission the patients by blows, strangulation, torture and sundry other punishments, is totally wrong, and we believe it was inspired by the enemy of God and men—Satan —and that such treatment may kill, not heal. We therefore do not demand that those institutions be reformed— they cannot—but rather transformed and managed on a novel basis, as explained in the last chapter of this book. And in this I am sustained by my own experience in insanity and the everlasting Word of God. But we say here, if those institutions were susceptible of reform, as managed by M. D's., Dr. Booth could do something in that direction. He seems, at least, animated by a disposition to do it. Dr. Booth let me speak to any patient, and without interference, let me judge for myself of the value of the patients' declarations. But in St. Peter asylum, Minnesota, Dr. Kilbourne, who accompanied me in several wards, denied or contradicted almost any statement of patients made against the employes or the institution, so far once I was obliged to tell him squarely that "I will find out myself if such thing is so or not." In the female wards of the Northern Wisconsin hospital, I met a woman patient, good humored and of a talkative nature, and after a brief talk with her, I only expressed my wish to speak for a few minutes alone with that patient, and immediately Dr. Booth drew back with the attendant. On several other occasions he let me freely speak alone with the patients. Well, I tell you 'tis fair dealing for an insane hospital doctor. In St. Peter asylum, I met a citizen of Minneapolis, detained therein as a patient. The man was clean and apparently intelligent, I gently pushed him into a bedroom right beside us to speak privately therein with him. But Dr. Kilbourne followed us. Then I told him: "Doctor I wish to be privately for a few minutes with this man. And he answered: "I run this institution and I won't leave you alone with him." Twice I requested it, and twice he refused. Then I commenced to inquire about the treatment of the patients by the employes and this intelligent patient had the courage to tell me in presence of the doctor, that he had seen the patients abused and showed me one of his fingers which had been broken by the employes. I asked the patient, "How?" "In throwing me down on the floor," he said. When far away from the patient, Dr. Kilbourne told me that this patient's finger had been broken by another patient. I don't believe it but let the investigation establish the truth about it.

Finally while we know that investigation is needed in the Northern Wisconsin hospital, and most probably in like manner, in Madison hospital, where we have not been, we see it is just as much needed or still more necessary in the two Minnesota insane hospitals. Of course we wish we could have been to Madison, and seen some other insane hospitals in some other states besides. But what we have done is about all our means could permit us to do under the circumstances.

But *en resume* if investigation is badly needed in the Wisconsin and Minnesota insane asylums, it is to be presumed that it is necessary in almost every insane hospital of the land to ascertain the iniquities of those infamous houses and to speedily stop all maltreatment of those unfortunates.

But now how is it ? The people of this country, in spite of their defects are generally, generous, good hearted. They have created societies for the prevention of cruelty to animals; and how is it, that they have thus neglected having their insane humanly treated?   Only one thing can account for it: There are the declarations of the doctors and managers of those hospitals who have constantly, (read their reports,) represented those hospitals as homes, residences for the insane, while the truth is that those unfortunates are therein beaten, kicked, strangled, tortured. knocked down and so forth. and are many of them, in a worse condition than slaves and prisoners.

Now from what has been said, we may also learn this important lesson, viz: Whereas the devil renders people insane by his infernal, crafty power, the doctors cannot cope with Satan. whether they bear the name of Kempster, Wigginton, Booth, Bartlett, Bowers, Gray, Ray, etc., etc. But now those at the head of insane hospitals are placed in the singular necessity of showing that they know something about the trouble.   Hence their senseless statements and blind treatment!   I have heard doctors and employes in insane hospitals lying simply as charlatans, and their treatment proved by itself to be sheer charlatanism, and can be nothing else in view of the nature of the cause of the trouble.   Whence the absolute necessity of stripping those doctors of the robe of imaginary knowledge with which they cover themselves and show them to the people just as they are in the true light.   The very nature of the case demands it. And from this exposé there can absolutely result but good for all concerned, including the doctors themselves. Glory be to God!

CHAPTER VII.

RUNNING OF THE HOUSE.—PATIENTS ABUSED.

A remarkable thing in the Northern Wisconsin hospital is that one would think that this house has been built for the benefit of the employes, not for the patients, judging from the conduct of the employes toward the patients. Thus, in the morning you hear in the ward the attendants halloo with an air of authority very much greater than the boss of a gang of wage laborers: "Knapp, Hanson, McGregor, go and make beds, Keily, Stemper, run the swab. McGuire, Redeemer, * run the sand-bag. Some other patients are sent to wash and scrub the floor, while others wash the dishes, and others are sent to some other occupations.

What they call sand-bag, is a big woolen bag filled with sand, weighing, it seems about 150 pounds. It is dragged on the floor by two patients, to make it shine, as mules draw the harrow on the field. Yes, and those patients forced to drag it become very warm, sweating, go out walking, and going out in that state of perspiration in winter, in the cold frost and snow, it is not surprising that they catch bad colds from this source. One day, considering the use of that sand-bag, some would say, "Accursed bag" and indignant on account of their making drag it a poor feeble patient who certainly rather needed rest and strong

---

*All those names are real names of real patients at the time in ward 9 S.

food, I told the first attendant of ward 9 S: "Your
sand-bag is a burden put on the patients' shoulders, without necessity, that neither doctor nor supervisor, nor attendant would move with his own fingers." A good, efficacious way for the people to stop the dragging of the
sand-bag, would be, I think, to compel it to be dragged in
like manner by the doctors and employes, for it is impossible to prove that it is more necessary or profitable to
certain patients who are obliged to drag it, than for the
doctors and employes! Hence the measure advised here is
rigorously just and equitable!

Then a grave question to examine in this hospital is the
work of the patients. We read in a certain old report of
this hospital: "Those of the inmates who are able and willing to assist in any of the departments of the farm, garden,
kitchen or laundry, etc., are permitted to do so, care being
taken that only a limited amount of work is permitted."
That is not true, now at least. It is a lie. The truth is,
that they compel the patients in many cases to work
against their will. Listen: Once in ward 3 and 4 S. I
saw the first attendant ask a patient to go with him
to do something. And on the quiet refusal of the patient
to accompany him, he violently cuffed the patient.
Another time I saw two other keepers ask a patient out
in front of the hospital to go and do some work, and as
he refused to go there, they forced him to do it, after having maltreated and beaten him. I know some attendants
who are always ready to get done by violence what the
patients will not do. I have seen once a sensible patient
of ward 9 S. sent to work in the kitchen for several
months totally against his will by the supervisor, acting
he said, by order of the doctor superintendent. Another
patient once told me that the attendants had threatened
to drag him to his work by the throat, if he refused to go

there.—Also many patients are doing a day's work almost as some wage laborers. They are called to go to work in the morning right after breakfast, (about 7 o'clock) and come back to the hospital after half-past eleven; and are called again to work very often before one o'clock, and come back to the wards ordinarily after five o'clock. Now there are some patients who work the seven days in the week and the 365 days of the year. Those are thus deprived of the necessary and beneficent rest of the seventh day. which the Creator has instituted for the greatest good of his creatures. I have seen as many as three patients at once, in our sole ward 9 S., who thus work for a long time the seven days of the week. Let there be promptly given a day of rest per week to those unfortunates.

Then in the name of all that is true, honest and reasonable, we demand that the names of all the patients alive, who have worked in this hospital, be carefully searched, to pay to each one of them, what is reasonable for his labor. In fact. citizens, the sole excuse that may be alleged not to pay them the fruit of their labor, is because they have lost more or less their reason. But because they are insane, incapable of defending or demanding their right, is that sufficient reason in your judgment to retain their salary, my brother? God forbid! Now to accept their work without any compensation whatever, as has been done so long here, and in some other asylums, is it not a glaring injustice? Therefore we demand that justice at least be done unto them. That those who earn. or have earned two shillings per day, or three, or four, or six shillings, or one dollar, or more, above their food and clothing, and the other useful expenses incurred in their behalf, all estimated at their real value, to pay them the same. Should it be found—who can tell—that

some individuals have profited by the patients' work,* let
the proper authorities, make those individuals pay
for that work, if it is possible. (For we all
know, that it is a great deal easier to let swallow,
than to make them disgorge). And if found that
it is the state that has profited by their labor, let the
state pay the patients for their labor. Let them be paid
for their work at all events. And what! my brethren, if
some are condemned in that day! for not having given
meat or drink to the hungered and thirsty, or not having
taken in the stranger, or not having visited the prisoners,
or not having clothed the naked. (AND THE SCRIPTURES
CANNOT BE BROKEN.) Of what greater chastisement shall
we not be judged worthy, if we deprive of their salary
our twice unfortunate brethren, who have worked, and
work yet in this hospital, and probably in some other
like institutions? And do you think we could escape the
condemnation pronounced in those words of God: "Go to
now, *ye* rich men, weep and howl for your miseries that
shall come upon *you.* Your riches are corrupted, and
your garments are moth-eaten. Your gold and silver is
cankered; and the rust of them shall be a witness against
you, and shall eat your flesh as it were fire. Ye have
heaped treasure together for the last days. Behold, the
hire of the laborers who have reaped down your fields,
which is of you kept back by fraud, crieth: and the cries
of them which have reaped are entered into the ears of
the Lord of Sabbaoth."—Now if it be found that many
patients in working from time to time, and rest part of
the time, have only made enough to pay their board,
clothing, etc., all estimated at their real value† it will also

---

*Was it ignorance or rapacity that moved him, I do not know; but once, I
saw the doctor superintendent in ward 10 S., try to get to work a poor, infirm patient, who could hardly walk.

†See Chapter VIII of this book about it.

be found that some other patients have worked continually for months and years, and several of them the seven
days of the week, without rest or intermission, until now,
or until the time they could happily get out of the hospital, in some way, and that without any pecuniary compensation whatever, although perfectly entitled to some
remuneration for their labor.   Therefore we believe, it is
high time to do them justice, lest those very words of the
mouth of the Omnipotent One be directly applied to us
also: "Woe unto him that buildeth his house by un-
righteousness, and his chambers by wrong; that used his
neighbor's service without wages, and giveth him not for
his work." For if such words are not applicable to those
who keep some patients laboring continually, sometimes
for years in hospitals, and after this send them away
exactly in the same state of mind as when they have commenced to work, without any salary at all for their work,
it would surely be difficult to see to whom they may be better applied.

Now in the wards of the most insane, we have seen
that the patients deprived of almost all right, are reduced
to a state of hard bondage. In many cases, their condition is worse than that of prisoners.   Listen: The
writer, we have said, had caught in the hospital, a bad
eruption on the legs. He was sent by the doctors from
ward 9 S. to the first attendant of ward 5 and 6 to apply
on the said eruption a certain remedy, that this keeper
prepared himself, with gunpowder and other stuff, a re-
cipe he had from an old German woman, I heard.   And
one day, the patient seeing in the hands of the attendant ready to apply the remedy, a small bottle of medicine,
ventured to ask him what it was.   The attendant answered him sternly: "It is none of your business." And
the patient asked him, (as in fact in the case it seems

come to that) "Do you believe you can poison me?" Thereupon, the keeper got mad, chased the patient out of the room, calling him crazy, and continued to maltreat him by harsh words. While the attendant paid in the hospital, to soothe the patients, sought by this mean and senseless conduct to excite the writer. he, on this occasion as on so many others kept calm and said nothing out of season. Necessity was made him the next day to tell all to Dr. Pember, and he did. But the doctor did not utter a single word of reproof with respect to the guilty attendant. And why should he while the same attendant commits the same and worse infractions of the rules under the doctor's eyes? Once the patient writer had written a letter in French to his wife, (Feb. '85). He agreed to read the French letter in English to Dr. Pember, provided the doctor would keep to himself the letter's contents. Thus the doctor entered with the patient into the first attendant's room to hear the reading of it. The first attendant entered with them in the room against the simplest rules of decency. The patient in seeing the intruder remarked to the doctor he wanted to read his letter to him alone. The doctor said the same to the attendant. But that was too much for this proud attendant not to resent. Upon some explanations that the patient gave the doctor about the letter's strange and mysterious contents, the doctor changed his mind, said he did not wish to hear the reading of it, he got up and went out of the room. But forthwith the attendant with his wounded feelings violently put the patient out of the room, giving not even time to pick up his papers, under Dr. Pember's eyes, who did not reprove him in the least. One day one of the patients in ward 5 and 6 was speaking. The first attendant told him to keep still. He did not. But the attendant thrashed him with blows on his bench. I thus take some instances from many others. One evening another patient was singing, seated on his bench, maybe a little too loud. The third attendant told him to stop and as he did not stop he violently cuffed him on his head. But all that is very little compared to what follows.

Reader, the things that we are going to narrate are very sad indeed. Our work of narration here resembles much the work of the sculptor, charged to make the statue of the goddess PAIN, spoken of by Lamartine. When the artist had achieved his work he was himself afraid of it. He threw a veil on her face. In fact who would not for the honor of this New Land beneficent, hospitable, courageous, generous, where any industrious workingman may come and find liberty with remunerative wages, and wherein almost any economical workingman may "conquer his independence" by his labor? Who would not cover with the veil of an eternal forgetfulness, the recital of these outrages perpetrated day and night on the patients of the Northern Wisconsin hospital? Citizens, I wish I could. But how may the people know how the unfortunates are treated if no one tell them? And how would the people try to relieve them if they ignore their sufferings? No, after a serious examination of all things, we see but one way to come to the rescue of those unfortunates.—Publication. Publication is the remedy against abuses. Publicity is the safeguard of the people. The way of stopping evil is not to hide it, but to publish it. Therefore let us for once bring to the broad day light, the works of darkness daily performed here in the darkness!

We have seen admitted into this hospital, some men very little deranged who became entirely insane, some even raving maniacs, after some time of sojourn in this hospital, most likely on account of the senseless and cruel treat-

ment they have received from the employes.   Let us cite
some examples.   Nothing better than facts.   Facts are
facts.

At the time of our clamorous folly (March 1885) a man
of a certain age already, but strong yet, was admitted in
ward 3 and 4.   He had then reason enough to behave
generally very well all the time.   A man active and dili-
gent, he soon set himself at work, and worked much.   He
run that way for some time, but one day as he unhappily
insisted on getting some tobacco just before going out
walking, the new attendant mad at him, threw him down
so violently against the bench that the patient, bruised
in the face, was bleeding much.   The patient got out with
the crowd, but when the keeper saw how he bled, he
brought him back into the ward. A report of this outrage
was written by an intelligent patient and sent to the
doctor superintendent and the attendant was discharged
on this account, so it was told me.   But the harm was
done.   The patient, irritated by such treatment, got excitable and behaved a great deal worse, he was punished
more by the other keepers, and the more they punished
him the more turbulent he became.   Then in a short time
he was one of the most turbulent and least respectful
patients in all the ward.   Hating with a perfect hatred,
the house and the employes, he got so far as to resist them
squarely in the face, for which things I saw him thrown
down on the floor, beaten, and punished severely.   His
excitement, nourished by punishment almost never appeased.   We met him over one year after those things,
always in the same ward (only passed in the department
above) always turbulent, impudent, insolent.   Thus became this patient from amiable, gentle and industrious as
he was when admitted to the hospital, most probably on
account of the cruel and inhuman treatment administered

here to him. This may be readily comprehended. Maltreat, strangle and strike a patient, as they do here, who generally believes that whatsoever he does, he is doing right, and nine times out of ten you irritate him, and move him to do some follies which he would have never thought of doing had he been charitably treated; then receiving again some fresh punishments for these follies, he gets worse and worse, and thus is literally fullfilled those words. "It is not here the place to get well, but to get crazy." We speak here about cold facts!

Ah! gentlemen, administrators of this house, who shall ever be able to make you comprehend all that is cruel, inhuman and senseless involved in the principle of submitting the insane to the will of their keepers! And who shall ever be able to calculate the disastrous consequences of this system? Eternity alone shall reveal it. For if we "Sow to the wind, we must reap the whirlwind."

At the time we write these lines,* that patient is yet in the hospital, more crazy than when admitted fourteen or fifteen months before.

Some time before the admission of that one, we saw admitted into the same ward a patient young yet, in all his vigor, who was so sensible at the time, that before two weeks had elapsed, he was sent from that ward into a better ward. There it appears he committed a little indiscretion. They maltreated him. He got mad. He was punished and got more excited. The next day he was sent back by the doctor to the worse ward, 3 and 4, whence he came. Here, excited to violence and meanness by the senseless behavior of the employes towards him, the patient was led to commit some acts of great folly and violence for which once perpetrated he was so punished and

---

*This book was written while I was a patient in the Northern Wisconsin hospital, but it was translated, revised, corrected and added to according to circumstances after being liberated.

treated as perhaps a wild beast could be. Afflicted, suffering, miserable, this patient is yet in the hospital, over thirteen months after those things, and more insane than when admitted into this house of woe! fifteen or sixteen months before. In view of all the injustice, cruelties, and folly of the treatment he has received in this house, the great idea of this patient is that a detachment of the U. S Army must come, take possession of this building, release the patients, and imprison the guilty parties. The last time I spoke to him (June, 1886) he cherished yet that idea, and hoped to be released that way. Poor fellow!

Listen: During the summer of 1885, a young man more or less intelligent and possessing certain knowledge, was admitted in ward 9 S. He was gentle, often amiable, and really little deranged. Some time after his admission, one afternoon, he went and quietly sat down beside some patients of another ward out on the ground in front of the hospital, at a small distance from our crowd. The then first attendant of ward 9 S. who singularly enjoyed the pleasure of making the patients submit by violence went there and commanded him to come back into our crowd. The patient did not respond right away to the order. But this keeper seized him and tried to bring him back by violence. And the patient resisting, there was fight. The attendant had both of his shirt sleeves torn to pieces in the struggle. But aided by the second keeper, who ran to his assistance, they violently brought back the patient and came to the very bench where I was sitting. The first attendant commanded him imperatively to sit on the bench. And the patient, more calm and reasonable than the keeper, at this moment at least, answered him, "I will sit down if you give me the time to do so, like a man." But instead of that he violently threw the patient on the bench, threatening him with further punishment. After this *bel*

exploit, the attendant went and changed his shirt. From this
cruel and inhuman treatment, it naturally resulted that
the patient, more or less proud, commenced to hate this
first attendant. He preferred hell rather than living with
him, he said. He received more punishment. He hated
more the house and its employes. And a few weeks later,
after having been cruelly beaten and strangled for some
deeds of folly, he was transferred, completely out of his
mind, and a dangerous maniac, into one of the worse wards.
He passed there the rest of the summer, then the autumn,
out of his senses.

Now having regained again more or less his reason, he has
been brought back again into a better ward. But one
year after his admission he is yet in the hospital. Now it
appears that this patient, reasonably treated, could have
been discharged after a very short sojourn in the hospital.
So thought the doctor it was told me. You see reader,
how the attend.nts here help the devil in his work. The
devil renders men insane, we have seen. And the keepers
actuated by Satan's spirit, from a little deranged that
some patients may be, make of them raving maniacs, by
their cruel and senseless treatment. "Satan casts not
Satan out!"

But listen again to an example of this kind. Here in
our ward 9 S. was last winter (1885-6) among the patients
a young man not much out of his senses. He was quiet
and meek, behaved well enough, only he happened to stay
in bed in the morning after the other patients were up.
On the Sunday morning, the 28th of February, 1886, this
young patient was yet in bed at breakfast time. One of
the attendants went and got him up, and brought him
down into the dining room. I saw that the patient
looked as having been maltreated. And the next day I
asked him to tell me, in my room, just what had happened

the previous morning.   And he told me that the attendant had first struck him in his bed, then he had thrashed
him with blows in getting down the stairs, which led from
the sleeping rooms down into ward 9. and that he had
continued to beat him along the hall, in bringing him into the dining room.   And in the forenoon of that day
(it was a Monday) we saw the same patient thrown on
the floor by the keepers.   The second attendant struck
him and wanted to strike him more.   But the first keeper,
more prudent, seeing us watching the scene, told him to
stop.   After that. the same boy was again punished and
beaten.   And a few weeks later this young man was transferred to a worse ward, in a quite miserable condition of
mind, greatly more insane than when he was adm'tted
to the house, about six months before, we think.   These
are facts which fully demonstrate the truth of this saying
of an ins ne—sane on this subject: "This is not the place
to be healed, but to get crazy. Humbug, Humbug." Humbug indeed.   I say here the truth, after having known
the true cause of insanity, and seen the remedies employed
in this house, to deliver the patients from their folly—
from their demons—and the general treatment of the patients, and the visible ignorance of the doctors in regard to
insanity, I then looked at this institution called a curative
institution of the insane, as one of the greatest humbugs
of this century, and I declared it to the friend whom I could
the most trust in the hospital.

   And how should not the patients get worse here?
Listen: During the summer of 1885, there was in this
hospital, an aged patient, apparently over seventy, and
more or less out of his mind.   But when let alone he was
more or less calm, and behaved tolerably well.   Only in
his irritable state of mind, when they vexed or annoyed
him, he got very excitable, and almost violent.   He swore

and cursed. And lo! the attendants themselves, almost all that came in contact with him, commenced to vex and torment him in sundry ways for their amusement. Sometimes they exasperated the old man in jesting about his family or affairs; sometimes they took his coat and made him run after them to get it back. At times they pursued him with some very disagreeable object. The old man exasperated, swore and cursed, at which the attendants amused themselves exceedingly. One day, a virtuous patient reproved an attendant in regard to this. And the senseless keeper responded, that "that old patient could not be cured any-how." (literally.) I saw those things taking place during the summer and autumn. And the old man died the next winter. He was buried, I think, the 26th of December, 1885. Poor old man!

But who could get an idea of the hardness of heart of these employes, if their deeds were not related by those who have seen them at work? A truthful patient and of sound mind told me, that once, there was a patient in his ward accused of abusing himself. The keeper had applied on the sexual part of the patient a burning medicine to stop him, in such quantities, that it had eaten up the flesh, so far as to perforate it with small holes. The patient overwhelmed with pain, swore that if any attendant would come again to apply the medicine, that he would certainly kill him. And the keeper ordered his colleague to apply again the medicine that evening. Whether it was applied, or not, I don't know. This patient, a man in all his strength, died in the hospital, during the autumn of 1885. He is now confined in the silent grave.

A patient in ward 3 and 4 was so completely out of his senses, that he would not walk, and almost all the time they dragged him where they wanted him to go. And while he was thus dragged on the floor, as some merchandise of very small value, a patient who is doing the attendant's work was kicking him, though that could not help him to go faster, while they dragged him. Of course, they beat him also on some other occasions. And every time he saw they were to strike him, oh! how pitifully cried out this poor innocent creature. But that did not stop them striking him. The devil who actuates them, has no pity. I know Satan surely, and them too. This patient was thus maltreated for a little while, after which he died in the hospital about the middle of April, 1885, it was told me. Could he live?

One Sunday morning, in November, 1885, the first attendant of ward 9 S. went down, with the patients, into the basement, where they used to go to put on their shoes, before walking out. And as one of the patients—a man very meek and quiet—could not find his shoes, the attendant ordered him to put on another pair in a hurry. And as the patient offered some objections, the attendant grasped him by the throat and strangled him. The patient cried out that some one go and call the supervisor to rescue him. And one sensible patient, really fearing that the attendant, in rage as he was, would choke to death this innocent victim, quickly ran to the doctor superintendent's office, and told him about it. Immediately after, when he knew that the report was correct, the doctor superintendent discharged the guilty attendant. It was high time. For this keeper, with his pride and violent temper, abused almost daily the patients. He nevertheless was for long months first attendant in ward 9 S.

On another Sunday, a little before that, one of the patients of ward 9, after the religious service, stopped and sat down on the stairs beside the garden gate at a little distance from our crowd, gathered on the lake shore. A keeper of another ward ordered him to come into our crowd. And as the patient did not quickly obey his order, he seized him, threw him down and strangled him. Then came the first attendant of ward 9. The patient was strangled again. And after having thrown him down and choked him several times, and shamefully treated him, they brought him back into our ward. A little while after came the two assistant physicians, who were taking a walk towards the lake. And as they saw this patient lying on the ground, Dr. Pember asked what was the matter with him. And while the keepers answered, one in one way, and another in another way, a sensible and courageous patient said, "Doctors, gentlemen, I will tell you what is the matter with Mr. Knapp" (the name of the maltreated patient.) Then he proceeded to tell the doctors, how, when the patient was quietly seated on those stairs, doing no harm to any one, the two attendants had violently brought him back, after having thrown him down several times on the ground, and strangled him on different retakings. Then he proceeded, telling Dr. Pember, (Dr. Craig had gone away) about the infamous conduct of the attendants, specially on the lake shore. He told him how the attendants' behavior, with their cursing, profane language, and the rest, was a great deal worse than the patient's conduct. And he told the doctor of the necessity of having some commissaries appointed to watch over the attendants' conduct. Dr. Pember listened through it all, but he did not address the least reproof to any of the guilty attendants, and none were discharged. As soon as the doctor had gone away, the first attendant of ward 9 told the patient Knapp, he would be strangled again.—In fact I have seen the same keeper throw violently three or four times in the same week, this same patient out of the clothes room, for the sole reason that he did not take out quickly enough his clothing and get out. I have seen him treat almost every day another quiet patient in the same way, and worse too. I have seen him on the ground by the lake, throw down another quiet patient, and strangle him several times, aided by the second attendant, because this patient had not come back into our crowd just as soon as ordered. I have seen the two same keepers throw down on the floor of ward 9, strangle, and severely punish a poor patient, very insane, because he, in some way refused to do, I think, the work they commanded him to do.

One day, during the autumn of 1885, we saw a small patient, of one ward stopping beside us, on the lake shore, run away as fast as he could. An attendant ran after him, caught him and brought him back. But before taking him back into the crowd, he threw him down beside the garden gate, and kicked him violently. A little while after, this same patient attempted once more to escape in running away. The same attendant pursued him, caught him again, and threw him down and kicked him as one would kick a wild beast.

On the 9th day of February, 1886, about 10 o'clock, a.m. a small patient, very meek and peaceable, of ward 10, tried also to run away on the Oshkosh road, about one mile south of the hospital, while walking out there. He was caught by an attendant of his ward, who forthwith strangled him, then cuffed him and kicked him. He then brought him back into the crowd where he again maltreated him.

On Sunday, the 25th of April, 1886, about 10 o'clock a. m., a patient of ward 9, attempted twice to escape on the road southwest of the hospital. The second time he was caught, he was brought back by the neck, by a keeper. And arrived where he wanted him, he threw him down on the ground.

Afterwards that patient tried to escape again and received more punishment. Then he was sent into one of the worse wards, to punish him. Having tried again to escape, one of the attendants then led him out to walk, with a strap, as a horse or dog, and when arrived on the ground where the ward stopped, the keeper bound him to a tree, with the strap. until the time of returning to the ward. Don't wonder too much about it. I have seen this summer (1886) the keepers of ward 5 and 6, bind together, day after day, with a strap two patients, because they had attempted to escape. And the ground where are so treated and strapped those unfortunates, is called the ground of recreation, by the managers of this house!! And they say that those recreations and the walks out doors promote greatly the health of the patients. That the attendants who do out doors all they wish, amuse and recreate themselves, I surely grant you gentlemen! But if you mean that the patients enjoy what you call walks, led out between two keepers as a herd of cattle, and kept, watched over, without necessity, as they are upon your so-called ground of recreation! then right here, I agree no more with you! For I have been thus led, kept, watched over during about fifteen months, and now I frankly declare to you that we have found no pleasure in it.

But to return to our run-away patient. I have seen him thus led and bound to a tree every day so long as I staid in the hospital. (June 23d, '86). Then after being liberated, I learned in Stillwater, Minn. (August, '86) that this unfortunate had thrown himself into Winnebago lake, while on board the excursion steamer, and was drowned! Poor young man! After many unsuccessful

attempts to escape on dry land, he threw himself into the
waters! The hospital living was unbearable to him!

Many other times, we have seen some other patients attempt to escape. That happens very often. In fact, we
may safely say, that as a general rule, the patients' pre-
dominant desire, is to get out of this house, in one way or
another. Now, no doubt the patients try to escape, because they don't like the house. Is it not then evident
that to beat, kick and strangle them when caught, just
causes them to hate yet more the house, and its employes,
and thus induces them to attempt to escape again? Then
the attendants who thus punish them don't know enough
to properly drive cattle, for the good cattle drivers, caress
the run-away oxen, when they catch them, to hinder
them from running away again.

On Monday, December 28th, 1885, we saw a small patient out of his mind, violently thrown down on the ice
of the highway's ditch in front of the hospital, and there
for several long minutes brutally cuffed and kicked, by
two attendants of ward 11 and 12. It appears they thus
treated him because this unfortunate had showed resistance. The courageous patient spoken of, had seen it all
also, and a few days later he made a complete verbal report of the affair to both Dr. Craig and the supervisor
Anderson. But the doctor did not utter a word of repre-
hension in regard to the guilty attendants, but rather up-
held their conduct, and of course neither of them was
discharged.

One evening, during the autumn of 1885, I heard a patient of ward 10, beside us, knock on his bedroom door,
then he knocked more and more violently, and was making a great noise. Then we heard a noise caused by
several men going in that direction. We heard the door
opened, then some screams as those of a man to whom

violence is done. We also heard a noise of fighting, and
this lasted for some time. A few days after, having met
that patient, I asked him what was the cause of that uproar such an evening. And he told me that after he got
into bed, he felt some intestinal pains, and that he
knocked at his door, to ask one of the attendants for some
medicine, and no one having come, he had struck the door
more and more violently. And hearing the uproar, the
keepers of ward 10, with some others, came into his room.
beat him very hard, strangled him, and after a hard and
cruel punishment, they brought him into a worse ward.
Strange treatment for intestinal pain indeed!

In a morning of April, 1886, I suddenly heard a
trampling noise in ward 10, which is separated from ward
9 only by a door. I went on and there I saw a big strong
patient held on the floor by the two attendants of that
ward. One of them kicked the patient hard in his side,
and the other was violently cuffing him. He that kicked
the patient (plainly out of himself) cried out for assistance.
In response to his hoarse cries, the two attendants of ward
9 hastened to his assistance, who at once started to strike
him too. They held him long on the floor, cruelly striking him. When all was finished, I asked an intelligent
patient of ward 10, what was the matter with this unfortunate, when they started to punish him. "All he
was doing," said this one, "was walking in the hall and
whispering, as he always does." In fact I knew that such
was the habit of that patient. Judge now of the bar-
barous means employed to quiet him! But of course they
did not calm him, for I saw him afterwards sent into the
worse ward of the hospital.

On Monday, May 24th, 1886, during the afternoon, a
patient of that worst ward 5 and 6, while he was with the
crowd of his ward on the lake shore ground, went and threw

himself into the lake. Some one hastened to his rescue and
saved his life. But when landed, a keeper of his ward beat
and punished the drowned man. The fact was reported to
us by several patients who saw it. Our ward was stopping
at the time at a certain distance from the lake. The attendant guilty of this outrage,left the hospital the next morning.
Whether he was discharged or left willingly,I do not know.

Another patient, what he had done I do not know.   I
only saw him brought bleeding into the wash room to be
washed there by another patient. He was bruised in the
face in such way, that he abundantly bled at the mouth
from the blows he had received for I don't know what
offence.   What I know is that patient behaved tolerably
well for an insane man as he was.

One evening this demoniac patient who pronounced my
name in Walloon, had come into the hall transversal.   I
don't know either what he might have done improper, but
certain it is that the first attendant grasped him by the
shoulder, to bring him into the other hall.   And as the
patient made a show of rebellion, the attendant precipitated him on the floor, and without loosing his grasp,
gave him, nevertheless, the chance of getting up.
When he got up, moved by the spirit of resistance,
he rebelled again, and forthwith the attendant precipitated him anew on the floor with his iron arm. And for
five or six times in succession, the patient was in that
manner violently precipitated on the floor. Thus he was
brought into the other hall.   Here, no doubt manifests itself the poor patient's folly (inspired in him by the evil
spirit) who causes him to resist to be thus crushed down
five or six times successively.   Here also manifest themselves the keeper's folly and cruelty, who repeatedly
crushed down this poor fool because he resisted him, instead of taking good care of him.   Both of them are fools

more or less dangerous. The patient more or less involuntarily. The keeper more or less voluntarily. Both
are actuated by the evil spirit, only in some different manner. The patient possessed of evil spirits is rendered insane by them. The keeper though considered as sane, is
nevertheless also animated by the spirit of error and evil.
His conduct proves it. He wants by all means the insane
to submit to his will.

Now it seems to us that those examples of maltreated
patients, just cited, fully suffice to give the reader an idea
more or less correct of the treatment of the patients more
or less out of their mind, in this hospital. Generally the
patients more intelligent are not so maltreated. As a general rule the most maltreated patients here are the most
insane and those of the poor class. But we must now say
that what we have related on the subject is only a part of
the facts which we have seen. We must also remark that
while a great part of the time locked up in a ward, we
generally could not see what occurred in the 27 other
wards, where very likely the same outrages were perpetrated to a greater or smaller extent.

Now should some citizens of Wisconsin doubt the truth
of the facts related, there is a simple way to convince
themselves of their reality. It is to proceed, by legal
means, to a serious investigation (as such investigation
ought to take place) and such an investigation must reveal some facts graver yet than any we have related. Only
how conduct this investigation is the question. For we
very well know that sharp reporters, judges or lawyers
may come, investigate the whole business and buildings
for long hours and see nothing wrong. Some relatives of
patients may come, and do daily come here, and after having been shown all the building, return home believing
that their loved ones are well treated and have here a

home! a residence! Listen: The first time my wife came
to the hospital, she was conducted by the Supervisor
Huntley all over the building before seeing me. During
that time my keepers put on me a new suit of clothes,
and fixed me up, for during my three last weeks of boisterous folly, my raiment had been torn by them and
was not yet replaced. Then, when introduced to me,
my wife said most sincerely, "You're well here, Frank,
you must like it under circumstances." "Dear," said I,
"I am here beaten, bruised, strangled." And I showed
her the eruption on my cheek. and told her its cause;
and told her of the companion I had for several weeks to
sleep with. She wept. . . . . But she had been so
cruelly deceived about the character of this institution,
that for the three subsequent years, she has stood by me,
prayed, worked, helped and encouraged me to put out this
publication, believing that it was a real duty for us to
show the people how the insane are treated in th's house
—to deliver them from their sufferings. Just what renders this state institution so awfully dangerous and
mischievous, is the diabolical craftiness of its managers
to conceal the evil from the visitors and investigators and
show them only what is clean, bright and beautiful. We
have pondered this question of investigation, and have a
plan laid out for the people to assure themselves that all
we reveal in this book is true, too true! and that even
graver facts exist. What is this plan? We keep it to
ourself until we see the people of Wisconsin ready, and
really in earnest to proceed to this necessary investigation. Then we will tell them our plan of investigation,
if they want to know it, to use it for the relief and
deliverance of our maltreated brethren.

For the present, citizens, let me rather tell you, as a
matter of fact, that, as once it was urgent to investigate

what transpired in the Romish monasteries, and submit
them to the control of the civil authorities, to protect the
inmates against maltreatment, and the abuses committed
therein, just as urgent now is it to investigate what daily
occurs in this hospital (and it is to be supposed in almost
all such institutions) and establish a sufficient control
thereof to protect the insane against maltreatment. For
we have seen what responsibility the doctors have, who
manage this house, in this maltreatment of the patients.
We have seen that the medical authority is to a great extent responsible for this state of things.* If the doctor
superintendents, have sometimes discharged attendants who
had abused the patients, this profits nothing, while they
keep right long in the service of the hospital, those attendants WHOM WE HAVE SEEN TREAT THE PATIENTS AS
WILD BEASTS. How could those doctors reform the per-
sonnel of employes, while one of the best disciplinarians
among them, Dr. Wigginton, himself declares: "Without
flattery, I think we have a very excellent corps of attendants, of which the institution and all concerned in
its management may well feel proud. (Second biennial report of the Northern Wisconsin hospital, page 142.) But
hear citizens, what was told me by one of the most sensible
of the patients, in the spring of 1885, after having been detained for several years in this house: "If the people of
Wisconsin, he said, should know what takes place in this
hospital, they would come and tear down the building.
(literally.) Let us rather say, that, in such doctors and
keepers there is folly also, surely. A folly of quite another sort than the folly of the patients of course, but it is
nevertheless a furious, dangerous folly, which when arrived
at its climax, forces to this conclusion, certain, necessary,

*Of course this does not exculpate the guilty keepers who have abused the
patients, while they should take good care of them.

inevitable, inexorable: Kill to heal!!   It is Satan's
wisdom. Kill instead of healing. I said so to the first attendant of ward 9. (March '86) Why! is it not to this
that the employes and doctors of this house must come
with their blind, and diabolical science and principle?
With such treatment, are not the patients necessarily
sent to the grave instead of being sent back cured to their
homes, and business?   And after a patient has been beat-
en, dragged, strangled, whipped, dropped, bruised. mocked,
vilified, maltreated and strapped down, as some are in
this house, is it not evident, that, (for the managers,) the
best place for such patient is the silent grave?   Is it not
evident that for them, the best place for me to go myself,
was the silent grave to bury there with me all the revelations contained in this book?   And who will be surprised that Dr. R. M. Wigginton, superintendent was very
anxious to have me sent back into Belgium, by the
Wausau authorities, at the time of my discharge from
the hospital.

Ah! in view of such treatment of these unfortunates.
we have cried to the God of Heaven. How long? oh! Lord,
how long? . . . And he will answer. He has already answered.   Is He not the God who takes care of the afflicted
and miserable? He has said so, and would He not do it?
Should the arm of the strong God, He, the only Wise, only
Good, Immortal and Almighty, the arm of the God of Abraham and Isaac and Jacob be shortened, that He could deliver no more? God forbid that we believe so. This second
folly would be worse than the first one. The deliverance
shall come for our brethren! Such is my trust in God!

Only let us keep in mind, citizens, that in such work of
relief, deliverance and salvation of our fellowmen, God
wants to make us workers with Him. And let me tell
you that while no letter of patients for outsiders ever gets

out without being inspected by the doctors, and that any
letter which speaks against the institution has no chance
to get out we have seen here the patients essentially, as a
general rule without protection. delivered up to the mercy
of their keepers. who treat them as shown in this book.
Let therefore the citizens provide for the patients as soon
as possible, in awaiting better things, the protection
against maltreatment which their deplorable situation in
this hospital demands, and in some others as we have
seen. Let those interested in the question see in the 15th
annual report of the State Homeopathic asylum for the
insane. at Middletown, N. Y., (1886) page 28 and 29, the
protection provided therein for the patients, by means of
a letter-box, placed in each ward. in which box letters for
the trustees may be dropped, by any of the patients, at any
time.*

Behold! Citizens of Wisconsin, we have shown you,
without hatred as without fear, how are treated in the
Northern hospital, our fathers, brothers, sons, and the
husband; and probably almost identically treated are our
mothers, sisters, daughters and wives. What are you
going to do? At any rate something must be done. As
for me, as long as the insane hospitals are not transformed, never, either the wife or child whom God has
given me, shall enter an insane asylum, while I can pre-

*In St. Peter asylum I asked Dr. Kilbourne from whom the patients could
get redress when beaten and strangled by their keepers. He answered me:
"I don't know."—To the same question Dr. Booth, of the Northern Wisconsin
hospital, answered me: "They can claim redress from me. No attendant doing
that can stay here." But the trouble is that every time a doctor passes
through the wards, he is, as I have seen, always accompanied by one or
several attendants; and how could the abused patient make complaint to
the doctor in presence of the attendants who have abused him, and may do
so again as soon as the doctor is out of the ward. This is so morally impossible that it never occurs. And thus I have seen the patients, in fact,
literally delivered up to the mercy of their keepers, without protection.—
Thus it is evident that the system of protection by means of those letter-
boxes in the Middletown Homeopathic asylum, is already a good improvement. Nevertheless, it is still insufficient, because a demented patient may
be abused for a long time before he gets sense enough to write a letter of
complaint and drop it in the box and as a general rule, the most maltreated
are always the most out of their senses.

vent it.   No, I love them too much, I have prayed too
much for them, to deliver them up into the hands of the
tormentors of insane hospitals! Of course I don't mean at
all that there is no danger in keeping the insane at home.
We know alas! too well that there is danger. But the
question is, because one insane perhaps in half a hundred,
(what do I know?) might be led to commit murder, ought
we to send all the insane to the tormentors of insane
hospitals?   For us we do not believe it, and thus we
have resolved to keep, if the case happen, our own
ones at home, after our experience of the treatment
at such institutions!

But now, it is evident that by thus settling the question
of *my* loved ones, that in no wise helps the unfortunates
locked up in this house.   And the same question presents
itself as before.   "What will you do for those maltreated
patients?"   Citizens, my brethren, we cannot help ourselves here!   It is for you from outside to come to our
rescue!   If we resist they do us violence, they torture us.
But when we extend to you our trembling hands, when
we show you our faces disfigured by bruise and torture,
when we show you our limbs hurt, bruised, broken by the
violence of the blows, will you refuse to come to our assistance?   American citizens, I tell you that I know
enough about your generous heart and character to feel
certain that if some speaker, even of doubtful probity,
should come this evening and tell you that in some remote
part of the world, in China or Japan, for instance, some
of our brethren were thus treated, you would send some
missionaries out there to relieve and deliver these afflicted,
if possible.   But now, I say you, hold on, stop. Do not
run to China or Japan just now.   Those things are taking
place in our midst, in the United States, in the civilized
state of Wisconsin, four miles north from Oshkosh, second

city in the state, at Winnebago, in the Northern hospital
for the insane. Citizens, I tell you that it is here that the
sufferers are from those outrages which I have suffered,
and seen some others suffer.

WHAT WILL YOU DO ABOUT IT?

At any rate, we hasten to add that we don't want any
aid by mob violence. We demand that the organized citizens proceed by peaceable and legal means to transform
those institutions so far as to make of them asylums managed for the good of the insane and NOT for the profit and
satisfaction of those who run them. We declare strongly
before all, that violence has been here done to us and our
brethren, without the least necessity. But we do not demand that violence shall be done to those who have in-
jured us. They have got outside of legality in regard to
us, 'tis certain. But we want to stay within legality in
regard to them. In treating us in that manner, surely
they have broken the divine, human and natural laws.
But now we demand that they shall be judged according
to the law. To add more illegalities to the illegalities
committed, would never re-establish legality. "Two
wrongs never made a right." At any rate we demand not
vengeance. We demand not the punishment of the culprits. We demand justice. We demand the deliverance
of our brethren the patients from all the wrongs by which
they are uselessly afflicted! in this hospital!!

This appeal was written over two years ago in the Northern Wisconsin hospital, in behalf of the abused, maltreated patients confined therein. But now we have seen
how, in like manner, same appeal ought to be made in favor of the unfortunates confined in other insane asylums.

CHAPTER VIII.

RUNNING OF THE HOUSE, CONTINUED—BOARD, CLOTHING.

Let us now come to the maintenance of the patients confined in this hospital. Let us first see what board they receive, and the real value of such board.

For breakfast the patients receive two or three days in a week, a little meat, beefsteak or sausage, with very little butter, and sometimes syrup, some bread and coffee and a potatoe. A couple of days a week, instead of meat they got fish, fresh or salt. Another day hash, and one day, Irish stew. There is generally oatmeal or boiled rice not sugared. Sometimes corn cake. And common crackers generally at every meal. Now, the days when the patients got some beefsteak, or sausage, if they had meat and butter enough they would make a tolerable breakfast. But it is far from it. Generally each patient receives a couple of small ball sausages. Some eating in the halls got only one. Now a person of ordinary appetite may eat three or four of those ball sausages, and this is so clear, that there is generally set aside enough for each employe to get that number of them. The beefsteak (without gravy) and fresh fish, are distributed to the patients in the proportion of the sausage. When, rarely, there are eggs, instead of meat or fish, each patient received a couple of them. The employes had set aside at least three or four or more eggs for each one of them. The great majority of patients eat at the table; and for those ones, in using the old pieces of bread, brought back from the previous meals, there is generally bread enough to eat. (Not so for those eating in the halls.) But it very often happens that a patient could eat yet, and as he has no more butter, nor meat, nor syrup—it is, in such case, only dry bread to eat—here the patient must cease to eat for lack of victuals. This remark equally applies to the supper, and sometimes to the dinner of the patients.

For dinner, the patients get two or three days a week some roast beef with gravy. (But the gravy being always cooled on the plate, not many patients eat it.) And some bread and potatoes. At noon the patients got no butter. Sometimes they got syrup. Ordinarily they got soup a couple of days a week! One of those days they get salt fish that many of them eat not. The other day they got neither fish nor meat. They get a piece of pie sometimes. One day a week there is corn beef, and rarely pork, fresh or salt. There is generally oatmeal or rice not sugared. One day a week some pudding, sometimes hominy. Sometimes cabbage, or onions, or pickles. But one must have partaken for a certain time of those dinners, without butter, even sometimes no syrup, without tea or coffee, but only cold water, to see how poor and cheap they are. But the supper of the patients is worse yet.

The supper properly consists of bread, with their beakful of butter, and tea. That's all; except that each one gets sometimes over this, only one cooky, or a very small piece of cake instead. Sometimes also each one gets a piece of cheese a little heavier than a butterfly's wing, all the same. Some days, too, they received at supper a little sauce or preserves (dried apples, peaches or prunes). For supper the patients never get any meat in our ward 9 S. Now we see that the employes, while the patients take this meagre supper, have some meat and always butter at will. And of those cookies, cakes, cheese, and prunes, peaches and apples (in sauce) it is visible that those three employes, served generally for themselves, as much of those things as is divided between ten or twelve patients, more

or less.—Every Sunday the patient's dinner consists of dry
bread, some beans, and mashed potatoes, with a small
piece of pie.   The patients got neither meat, nor butter,
sometimes even no syrup, nor tea nor coffee at noon on
Sunday. So it is at least in ward 9 S.   Now the ward 9
is the one where are kept the most intelligent patients,
except one, the ward 8.—To these general rules there are
a few exceptions.   Thus the patients who serve at the
table, at the meals that the patients got no meat, they
used to serve to themselves a good piece of meat.   Not so
foolish for supposed fools.   There is also a couple of patients in ward 9, who got some meat every day for supper
just as the employes.   Why? I don't know, except that
those patients are paying in part or in full, their board to
the hospital.   At any rate since there is given those
patients and the employes some meat and butter at every
meal, while the patients are deprived of it, at some meals,
it is a recognition of the fact, that it would be better for
every one to get some, and that it is cut off the patients'
meals by economy or avarice.   We clearly see, while the
patients got generally morning and evening, scarcely half
the butter they could eat, and got none at noon, that the
employes have three times daily, all the butter they could
eat and more. Also that while the patients are without meat
for dinner, the day they have beef soup, that that day the employes received very good looking fresh boiled beef, but
always all for them, the patients have none of it.   We
have also seen the share that the patients received of eggs,
sausage, beefsteak, etc. etc., and the share that the employes received.   Now in view of those facts, and in virtue
of the right that ought to give us our participation in the
expenses occasioned by this hospital, in the payment of
our taxes, every year at Wausau, we demand the doctors
and trustees of this hospital, to establish before the people

of Wisconsin, that the eggs, sausages, beefsteak, cheese, cakes, pies, dried prunes, peaches, apples, butter, boiled beef and gravy are doing more good in the stomachs of the employes, than in the patients' stomachs, or else if they cannot demonstrate that, to admit that they are judges with iniquitous thoughts! who govern this house to the profit and welfare of the employes against the interests of the patients.*

This request addressed to the doctors and trustees, we turn to the people of Wisconsin, and say to them: Citizens if such is your desire and will, to feed the insane as they are here, truly we have no complaint to make about it. We accept the board as it is, without any recrimination on our part, at least. But if you say that you are paying, to the state in your taxes, sufficient to provide reasonable and proper board for the patients of this hospital, as appears to be the case, then citizens, my brethren, I tell you that robbery is in vogue in permanency in this house. Then let the people generously take some small cords and make a whip, to drive the guilty parties out of the temple. We mean of course to get them out by legal means, without mob violence or riot.

But listen: Having kept account day by day, month after month for several years, of all the house expenditures concerning alimentation, we are able to see so well, we think, how much such or such board may cost per day per person, that we may safely say that the board as provided to the patients of the Northern hospital, does not amount to over 12 cents per day per patient. If the citizens of the state doubt the truthfulness of this assertion, let them have a committee of a few men thoroughly honest, ap-

---

*Of course so far as the doctors are concerned, those demands were addressed to Drs. Wigginton, Craig and Pember, then doctors in charge of the hospital, but inasmuch as the affairs in this r-spect are now on the same footing, they are just as applicable to the doctors incumbent.

pointed to take charge for a month at least of the hospital
boarding house, who will make, prepare and distribute to
the patients, during that month, such board as they have
received for all the time of our sojourn in the hospital, and
that they have probably received at least until our last
visit there (May 25, 1888) and if they keep a fair account
of all expenses, we confidently believe, they will surely
find out, that the cost of such board amounts to not over
12 cents per day, per patient.

Now at this rate of 12 cents per day, my board at the
hospital, for the 547 days of our detention in that house,
would only have amounted to the sum of $65.64. There
has been claimed from us, at Wausau, for our board in
the hospital, $99.00, that we have paid. Now let it be
well understood that those $99.00 are only the share paid
by the county for my board to the hospital; the rest which
amounted to about twice as much, must have been paid by
the state. In other words, while I might have eaten, during 18 months in the Northern hospital, about 65 dollars
worth, there has been paid by me and the state for my
board during that time, about $300.00 (three times $99
and some cents.)

Now if there is not need of investigation of the management of the affairs of this hospital, I don't know where
investigation is needed, surely.

Now how much the clothing may cost of the patients
yearly is a more difficult question to answer. Generally
the patients arrive here with more or less clothing, and
they receive none from the hospital until their own are
more or less worn out. Then there are some patients,
clothed in part or altogether by their relatives, or friends.
It is in that way that I received $7.00 worth only of
clothing from the hospital in one year and a half.* As

---

*We must state here that they lost or *stole* from us in the hospital a sum
of over $8.00 in clothing, consisting of drawers, under shirts, over-shoes,

far as the clothing of female patients is concerned, it must really cost little as they are clothed in calico in a great measure.

At any rate we see in the report of the hospital that there is carried to the expenditure of this institution, for clothing $7,800, for the year 1885; $5,900 for 1886, and that there is allowed for each of the years 1887 and 1888 $6,300 for clothing. Now in taking that average sum of $6,300 per year for clothing, for the number of 630 or 631 patients, kept annually on an average, male and female in this hospital, it would cost yearly for the clothing of each patient, on an average, the sum of $10.

Now the board at the fixed price of 12 cents daily, per patient would amount to $43.80 per year. And in adding to this sum the $10 for clothing, the cost of the maintenance of the patients, clothed and fed as they are in this hospital would not amount to over $54 in round numbers. yearly per patient on an average, for board and clothing.

Now in adding to this sum $10 more per patient, yearly, for heating, light, bedding expenditure, and the expenses of preparing food and taking care of the clothing, which appears to be a liberal allowance for those objects, the cost of the maintenance of each patient, clothed and fed as they are in this hospital must not exceed $64 a year.

It cost at Gheel, Belgium, 1 franc and 65 centimes daily per patient (which amounts to about $120 a year) for board, lodging, clothing and all the care taken of the insane included.

Let us state right here, that we see it has already cost the state and tax payers of Wisconsin up to $336 yearly

socks, etc. And in spite of there being no one single article lost through our own fault, and despite all the claims we made, we never could receive anything in compensation, but now on the other side, when I got out of the hospital a sum of $7.00 was claimed from me, at Wausau, and which I have paid, for clothing received at the hospital. Well if that is justice, it is insane hospital justice, no doubt. Now, sad to say, but true, I have seen some other patients fixed that way with their clothing.

per patient on an average, for their maintenance in this hospital, all expenses included of course, and that the least it has ever cost yearly per patient, is $167 on an average. (See second bi-ennial report of the Northern Wisconsin hospital, in the table, page 17.)

But now, citizens, to this lowest rate of $167 yearly per patient, there is yet paid, by the tax payers, $103 annually per patient, to keep them in this hospital, more than it would cost to keep them at home, so fed and clothed, since we have seen that that must not amount to over $64 annually, per patient. Now I tell you that to pay $103 yearly per patient to have them kept in this hospital, treated as they are treated, this seems a little dear, does it not, citizens? Yes, it does surely, but this however is but one side of the question. For if we now consider that a much greater number of patients are cured in the hospital receptacles of New Zealand, the most of them without doctors or medicines * than in this hospital: if we above all consider that while the doctors of the Northern Wisconsin hospital report 12 per cent. of recoveries † that the ratio of recoveries, at the colony of Gheel, Belgium. where they generally receive the most of incurable cases, and where the patients are taken care of by simple countrymen, amounts to 28 and 30 per cent. for the years 1886 and 1887, if those figures mean anything, do they not show up clearly, first that a patient who would be kept and taken care of at home, as the insane are at Gheel (save the hard work) would have two or three times more chances of recovery than to be sent to this hospital! and that we consequently pay $103 yearly per patient, to get them

*See "The Curability of Insanity" by Dr. Pliny Earle.

†See second bi-ennial report of the Northern Wisconsin hospital, 151 recoveries for the two years 1885 and 1886, on a number of 1,258 patients under their treatment during that period, table page 143.

kept and treated in this hospital, with twice or thrice chances less to be cured, than to be kept at home?

But let us look a little further. In some particulars received from Belgium we read that there are now at Gheel 1,300 patients. That the township is divided into four sections, and that a doctor with the derisive salary of 300 francs ($60) per year, is attached to each section, with an inspector.

Now each doctor of the Northern hospital received on an average a yearly salary of $1,120 (5,600 francs) if the sum of $4,480 annually allowed to them (four) were equally divided. But we see that the doctor superintendent takes of the total sum $2,300, then the first assistant gets $1,000. then there is $700 for the second assistant, and there only remains $480 for the lady physician;peculiar division of salary indeed!* If the salaries were thus divided between the four doctors of Gheel, the fourth one should live, he and his family of the pure air of Campine surely. And then blind is this division of salary, for certain it is that the doctor superintendent casts not one more devil out of the insane for $2,300, than does the lady physician for $480. But we must pass over this. We say that the four doctors of the Northern Wisconsin hospital, with a yearly average salary of $1,120 (5,600 francs) give us now 12 per cent. of recoveries, while the four doctors of Gheel. with a yearly salary of $60 each give from 28 to 30 per cent. of recoveries.

Thus the four doctors of the Northern hospital in giving us 75 recoveries per year† for the total salary of $4,480, we pay them for the recovery of each patient at the rate of $60 in round numbers, for doctor's salary above their board. And the four doctors of Gheel,in giving at the

---

*Since the above was written, the lady physician has been replaced by a third male assistant, with a salary of $600.

† See second bi-ennial report page 143.

average rate of 29 per cent. 377 recoveries on the number of 1,300 patients,for the total salary of$240,there is paid to them about 64 cents per recovery of each patient on an aver-age, and they board themselves, I think. That is, for the sum of $60, paid to the doctors at the Northern Wis-consin hospital, above their board, to have a patient re-stored to reason, the doctors of Gheel lead back to reason 93 patients, and board themselves, I think.*

Of course we don't believe in the science of the doctors to cure insanity. But now the doctors of the Northern Wisconsin hospital are necessarily placed in this dilemma, not pleasant indeed for their glory: They must grant us that the patients discharged as recovered have not recov-ered by their treatment, or else that their treatment as doctors' salaries, cost to the tax-payers 93 times what cost the treatment of the doctors of Gheel, without board. We had previously demonstrated, we believe, by reasoning that this institution was one of the greatest humbugs of this century, managed as it is. Now we have demonstrated the fact mathematically—by figures. And in view of those facts and figures, I do think that the reason, good sense and purse of the citizens demand strongly and unan-imously, that this institution for the insane be quickly transformed or shut up. It is a humbug. It answers not the purpose for which it was created It is not a simple humbug either. But a great, awful, disastrous humbug ! wherein our unfortunate fellowmen may lose their health, their liberty and life through maltreatment! In fact the idea that a person of good sense may get out of this hos-pital, after having been here a long time, is this: This

---

*Truly, it is less than two years ago that a lady physician was added to the three male doctors of the Northern Wisconsin hospital. But as this lady doctor received only $180 per year, out of the total sum of $4,440 paid annually to those doctors. this change cannot much affect our figures, nor much diminish the cost paid per recovery of patient, for all the time the hospital was run without a third assistant.

house, is, as a general rule, but a miserable place of detention for the more or less intelligent patients; a place of woe and torture for those out of their mind,* and an abode of princes for doctors and high officers. In fact it took a heavy pressure last summer (1887) to force one of those doctors out of the Northern hospital.

Another thing: while there is allowed the four doctors of the Northern Wisconsin hospital a yearly salary of $4,480† they visibly receive eighteenfold what the four doctors of Gheel receive, their annual total salary being only $240. Now while the doctors of Gheel have under treatment 1,300 patients when the doctors of the Northern Wisconsin hospital have generally less than 650 patients, this doubles again the salary of those last ones, making it, with respect to proportion of patients under treatment, thirty-six fold what the doctors of Gheel receive.

And yet there is not a very great difference in the cost of maintenance between the patients kept at Gheel and those kept in the Northern Wisconsin hospital. The cost at Gheel being generally $120 annually, and $167 now at the Northern hospital. And the doctors of Gheel who only receive, without board, the thirty-sixth part of the salary paid to those of the Northern Wisconsin hospital, above their board give twice or thrice as many recoveries as the Northern Wisconsin hospital doctors, though as a general rule, Gheel is the institution where the greatest number of incurable cases is admitted. And right here is the secret of the whole business: Not to give the money spent in behalf of the insane to the doctors who

---

*There are some exceptions to this rule. We have seen here some patients very well treated; and some persons of note or influence even having a special attendant to walk with them out outside of the crowd of their ward. Of course such have no complaint to make against the management. But that favoritism helps not the rest of the patients surely.

†Their yearly salary amounts now to $4 600, making it nineteenfold the Gheel doctor's salary.

CANNOT CURE the insane. It is certain that the doctors
can kill the insane, we have seen it; heal him, he CANNOT,
have we seen also in view of the nature of the trouble.
But a good, christian, devoted keeper may lead back the
insane to reason by the grace of God. Therefore here is
wisdom, here is the way to spend the money in behalf of
the insane: for good, devoted keepers, and not in doctors,
drugs, and all such appliances, or in foolish expenses of
supervision, all things that, generally speaking, cannot
cure or even relieve the insane.

CHAPTER IX.

INSANITY INCURABLE BY THE DOCTORS.

We have seen that while we were condemned by the
doctors, ready to die in their hands, in our folly, how we
have been permanently cured, in a moment, by the grace
of God, and a passage of Scripture. Glory be to God. We
have seen that our recovery cannot be due to the cruel,
inhuman, senseless treatment received at the hospital,
since such treatment proves itself to be but folly, cruelty, and sheer charlatanism. These are facts.

Now we really believe that this is, as a general rule, the
case of all the patients discharged as recovered from this
hospital, and others. They cannot have been cured by
the earthly, blind and senseless science of the doctors,
since they ignore completely what is the real cause of the
trouble. Wherefore, while the everlasting Word of the
Almighty and Omniscient God reveals to us clearly, what
is the real, immediate, effective cause of insanity and
epilepsy—Satan speaking and acting through the patient—
while we have clearly seen ourself the evil spirit speaking

and acting through the insane, we cannot hesitate for a moment TO PRONOUNCE INSANITY INCURABLE BY THE DOCTORS.

Therefore, based on such foundation that neither criticism nor argument, nor sophistry, nor theory, nor erudition, nor ignorance can ever remove, we say to any person who has any relative or friend smitten with insanity: Your loved one is possessed of one or several demons. Whether you believe it or not, there *are* demons— Christ declares it—and it is those demons who render insane our loved ones, by taking possession of them. Again, the Lord Jesus Christ has revealed to us this fact. Wherefore friend, any doctor who stands as a healer of insanity or epilepsy, ask him gently: "Doctor, have you received the power to cast out the demons as Peter, as Philip, as Paul, or any other of the Master's disciples?" And so long as he cannot prove his ability to thus cast out the demons, do not believe he can cure your loved ones, afflicted with insanity. The doctor is either deceived or deceiving you. He is a knave or a fool. He cannot escape this fatal dilemma. Of course we don't say that insanity is an incurable trouble of itself. No, many insane have been seen again, clothed and in their right mind. We only say that the trouble being produced by an invisible, impalpable, spiritual power, the cause therefore escapes all the senses and science of the doctors, and cannot be removed either by medical science or by any human power.

Now to any doctor who would contest this, we shall say in advance; for us we are nothing; but to prove we are wrong on this subject and that you can heal the insane by medical appliances, you must prove that the Lord Jesus Christ, the Creator of the soul, spirit and body was mistaken about the cause and cure of insanity and epilepsy, and the word of God to be untrue. 'Tis a hard task for a mortal man to perform, be he doctor or not!

Now it is evident in those conditions, that our insane hospitals become a great useless burden, a harm, a nuisance in the state. If those hospitals were built for the purpose of keeping and taking care of the insane therein, as the county insane asylums, the harm would be infinitely less. But, as all know, they are built for curative institutions of insanity, and provided with all the appliances that medical science could suggest. There are kept doctors with considerable salaries, to do the sad work that we have shown they do, at least in the Northern Wisconsin hospital. In regard to these expenses, we say the harm is comparatively small, because after all it is only a pecuniary loss endured by the community. But the harm is exceedingly greater, when it is a question of citizens, who have patients in this hospital, and for many unfortunates confined herein. (And this is equally true in regard to some other insane hospitals.) Listen: The insane are sent here, in many cases, with the hope that the doctors can cure them, while we have seen they cannot. Now citizens, see what evils flow from this fatal, ruinous error —to believe that the doctors can cure insanity. The insane person is sent and confined in this house, suffering, in many cases moral, mental and physical tortures, that only those can comprehend who have suffered them, on account above all (notice well this point) of the deprivation of their own dear ones, who could surround the patient with affectionate care, while he is here badly abused, without the least necessity whatever. It seems most certain to us, that so many unfortunates stay in this hospital suffering what they suffer here, treated as they are treated, because their relatives ignore their doom in this house of woe and torture, otherwise they would not let them stop here. Citizens, listen: To beat, strangle and torture the patients, and so forth, are deeds of darkness, surely, and generally—not always—those who commit those deeds hide them more or less. This we have seen. And when the patient speaks to his relatives, if he has a chance to see them, of what he suffers in the hospital, they generally do not believe him, because he is insane, although all that he says here is only too true. They think wrongly that it is some delusion. Then, if perchance they believe the patient has in fact been punished, then they think it had been necessary to punish him, for who after all, in possession of a mind and heart, would or could have ever believed that the employes can beat unto blood, strangle almost to suffocation, and bruise sorely the patients without the least necessity whatever? This, it seems to us, is the case of the insane, sent and left in the hospital by their relatives or friends. At any rate, here are, and stay the unfortunate insane, the sport and victim of the employes in many cases; and probably to the profit of the managers of this house. And this evidently, in many cases, on account of the fatal, ruinous error, which induce the people to believe, that the insane might get cured better in the hospital than to be kept at home. Now have we not demonstrated all the awful truth contained in those words of an insane, sane on this subject: "It is not here the place to cure, but to get crazy. Humbug, humbug." Humbug indeed, it is!

Now the worse of all this is, that the doctors and managers of this house endeavor to get the people to believe that the insane generally find here a home! Here they cannot escape the fatal dilemma. They are blind or hypocrites. They ignore how the unfortunates are treated in this house—this is a fatal blindness, or knowing it, they conceal the awful truth from the people—this is an alarming hypocrisy.

Then, if the doctors don't see their inability to cure insanity and epilepsy, after having drenched with their medicines some patients for years consecutively, without cure or improvement in their condition, what blindness!! And if they have seen it, why not proclaim their powerlessness to cure such patients in order that the people could see what they have to do, to do right with the patients? Let us hope now that the most honest among those doctors will do it!

Now citizens, you know, some of you at least, that a strong argument in favor of the creation, and maintenance of insane hospitals, is the cases of patients discharged, as recovered from those institutions. But you have seen that those cases of recoveries cannot be due generally to the treatment of the doctors. But supposing now for a moment that they could make of this, with good reasons, a sound argument in favor of the erection and support of insane hospitals; what argument, my friends, could not we make also against these institutions, of all those cases who come to the hospital in a state of mind more or less reasonable, and who become to the sight of the doctors and employes, crazy enough to do all kinds of follies, and sometimes become raving maniacs? And also of those cases, who after having enjoyed for a certain time more or less reason, become insane again, while under the treatment of the same doctors? If they tell me that these things occur to but a restricted number of patients in proportion, well I grant it. But those cases, all unfortunate as they are, so far, are not the most unfortunate admitted to the hospitals. It is another class—and they are not a small number—more miserable yet, because their doom is forever sealed down here. What is this class of patients? Ah! gentleman, defenders of those institutions, this class of patients are those who, once admitted out of their senses, or getting so after admission, are afflicted here with nameless, numberless pains, anguish and sufferings caused the most of it by punishments and useless restraints, as we have stated, and then die in the hospital! O men! imagine if you can what could happen worse to those thrice unfortunates if they had been kept and taken care of at home. Tell me. As for us we deem that this class of patients at least, would have gained much by being kept at home, at least all those who possessed a home. Some might probably have recovered, too! well treated at home.

Whence it appears clearly, that even if their argument drawn from the cases discharged as recovered, could be sustained in favor of those institutions, there are some grievances, too true, alas! that cry aloud against them! Moreover, if you send an insane person into one of the worst wards—real pandemonium—where there are already thirty-five demoniacs, more or less, where some violent among them may occasionally strike him, and he hears there the terrible yelling, screaming, crying, swearing and cursing at times; and sees all the signs and gestures of all those demoniacs, and is abused and maltreated as some patients are, and dosed, drugged by doctors, who all of them are a great deal more ignorant about the true cause and effects of insanity, than the insane themselves, if you can imagine a more fit place in the world for one to get more crazy you will render me service in telling, for truly we fail to discover it this side of hell.

Nevertheless we do not demand the abolition of those institutions, but we demand their complete transformation. In the nature of the case they must be transformed or shut. And if they don't want to do that, let all sensible, good hearted people keep their insane at home as we have seen some doing. That will give them a great many more chances of recovery, besides many other great advantages.

Citizens, I must also speak to you of another great harm in the state, apropos of these hospitals. Listen: When it is a question of judging a person whosoever it may be, of some crime or delinquency, you establish a jury of twelve men, by law, to judge if the accused person must be deprived of his liberty by imprisonment, or of a part of his property by fine: and we believe there is much good in the jury's institution, in spite of its defects, and so you do since you maintain it. But don't you see that we are 630 persons in this house of woe (and many more in some other hospitals) whose liberty—and even life are depending on the will of one man—the doctor superintendent? and that this man may as he does in fact—by his sole authority keep separated the son from his father, the daughter from her mother, and the husband from his beloved wife according to his will? But now, if this doctor is unjust or senseless, don't you see what a cheap bargain you make with our liberty and life? And don't you know that just men are so scarce that it were not possible to find ten just men within Sodom and Gomorrah to save them from destruction? Is the history of our race lacking in examples of bad kings, of senseless and unjust ministers, governors, administrators, or of blind doctors? On the contrary the world has never been lacking in charlatans! Well then since you have, at any rate played with the liberty and lives of the citizens of this state locked up in this house, permit me to tell you before the world, that at this very hour we are writing these lines in the hospital, (May, 1886,)* some persons sane enough to certainly make, if at large, useful citizens, working and producing, are de-

---

*And so was it May, 1888. On'y Dr. Booth told me after my representations in regard to this, that he proposed himself to send on furlough these intelligent patients.

tained in this house by the arbitrary will of the doctor superintendent.

Now listen to a little bit of true history: While we were working every day with our own hands at Wausau, Wisconsin, doing useful work for us and family, city and state, while we were loving and observing the laws of the country, we were striken with insanity and got crazy enough to kill, and in a moment of immense misfortune that most assuredly human science cannot comprehend, we mortally struck the dear, dying brother we loved as ourself.

Two days later I was brought into the Northern hospital to be cured of my folly, and then be returned to my family and society, work and business—thought my wife and myself as soon as I could think of anything. *All lure!* Arrived in the hospital the doctor superintendent reproved me sternly, because of my deed. Dr Craig sneered at me. And Dr. Pember helped to strangle me, to quiet me I suppose, for I found him the best of the trio. The attendants called me "murderer," told me I deserved to be hung, etc., and treated me as related. I was handcuffed day and night, and put into a crib bedstead to sleep. My handcuffs were only removed for the night, almost two weeks after my recovery, and after two requests of ours addressed to the doctors to this effect. And I was put into an ordinary bed to sleep over *a month* after my recovery and at my request. Being yet detained in the worst ward—5 and 6—over six weeks after my recovery, I asked Dr. Craig (end of May '85) to be changed of ward, he told me, "No."—I asked him why, and he said, "Because your deed deserves twenty years of penitentiary."—And time and again Dr. Wigginton told me I had committed a bad deed.—We know that in that awful moment, the devil, through us,

committed a terrible crime.   But by what right—I do
ask—do those doctors and keepers make themselves judges
in my case?—I was only changed of ward the next month,
almost two months after my recovery, and after another
request. The 17th day of June, '85, my wife came and
visited me at the hospital, for the second time. She found
that the best place then for me would be at home. I told
Dr. Pember so. He declared, if it was not for my deed, I
could be discharged then from the hospital; but I had
better speak of those things to the doctor superintendent.
A few days later I told Dr. R. M. Wigginton, superintendent, that my wife, judging me well enough, wanted
me home. He told me he would do the best he could for
me, but he could not let me go then. In August, my wife
came again, and finding me well, on her return home, she
wrote to Dr. Wigginton that she had known the patient
writer for the last past fourteen years, that she had been
married for twelve years to him, and that always he behaved himself as a real honest man, good husband, and
good citizen. But that in taking care, day and night, of
his sick brother (who got very insane at last) he unfortunately got insane like him, and while completely out of
his mind he had committed the deed he knew.   But now
that again in full possession of his reason, she was assured I could hurt nobody, or if there was some danger
she would certainly be herself the first in danger.   She
further offered to put in security for me all we possessed,
and she prayed the doctor superintendent to let me return
home on bail or otherwise.   Dr. Wigginton refused to let
me go.   But again, in the next month (September), my
wife wrote once more to the doctor superintendent, asking
him to send me home, and offered again the same security.
This time Dr. Wigginton not only refused to send me
home, but refused my wife permission to visit me.   And

he told me to write my wife to bother him no more with
my discharge, that my case was too bad, and he told me
then and several times besides, that if *he* would let me go,
the county judge would not permit it. But when at last,
my wife, on the advice of Dr. Wigginton, went to the
Wausau county judge, the judge told her: "Your husband
has been sent to the hospital as insane, and declared such
by two Wausau physicians. I have nothing to do with
his case. The doctor has no right to keep him there
well." This overthrew completely, the sayings so often
repeated by Dr. Wigginton about my case and proved
that I was detained in the hospital against law and reason,
by the sole authority of Dr. Wigginton. Thus, well,
and in full possession of our reason—the three doctors of
the hospital saying so—we were detained in the hospital
until the 23d day of June, 1886, over fourteen months
after our recovery, by the sole authority of Dr. R. M.
Wigginton without judgment or condemnation, in flagrant
violation of the constitution which proclaims that: "No
person can be deprived of life, or liberty, or property,
without due process of the law."

And very likely I would have stayed therein long
months, perhaps years more, who can tell? if I had not
the most innocently worked my way out. Listen: Knowing what was the true cause of insanity—Satan—once
when opportunity came, I told Dr. Pember: "I know,
doctor, you don't know much about insanity." And a
little while after I told Dr. Craig: "Doctor, your position
as physician here is specially curious, because you don't
know what is the cause of the trouble of the patients
under your treatment." Then a couple of weeks later, I
told again Dr. Pember: "Doctor, the declaration of Dr.
Craig about the cause of my headache, is a pure and simple
condemnation of your treatment for the past eight

months." And he admitted it. At the same time, I gave
Dr. Wigginton to clearly understand, by my behavior,
I had no faith in his science, nor advice. I requested him
to discontinue to me such medicine; he blamed me for
reading my Bible too much, and I kept reading it diligently every day. He wanted me to go to dances, and I
never went to dance. He wanted me not to read
such books, and I did read those very books. He wanted
me to go working out and I stayed in reading and writing.
Further, the three doctors had several times assured me
that they were doing and would do the best they could for
me. But once I asked the doctor superintendent the permission to let me go with my wife, and under supervision.
to Oshkosh to buy me a suit of clothes for holidays; he
did not even answer me. He refused to send of my own
money the price of those books I wanted to buy. He once
refused to send a despatch to my wife at my expense.
Then seeing I was detained in the hospital by his sole
authority, against his promises and delarations to me, and
realizing finally I had to deal with doctor hypocrites who
had fooled me right along, I told Dr. Pember: "Doctor, you have never been sincere with me." He protested.
And I told him: "Doctor. you, nor Dr. Craig, nor Dr.
Wigginton, have never been sincere with me. Tell it
to your colleagues." "How do you know it," he inquired.
"I judge you upon your deeds and words," said I. This
was probably all they could stand. For Dr. Wigginton
came into our ward and told me to do my work in the
ward and keep still, not to speak so much. I readily understood what he meant, and answered him: "Doctor, I am
just doing that way for over one year, I have recovered my
reason." He kept still. But he had clearly perceived I
was getting very inconvenient in the hospital, and when my
wife came he sent her to the county judge for my discharge.

This brief history of our detention in the hospital shows up how a citizen may be detained here (judged by doctors and keepers who have no legal power to do it) against his wishes and the wishes of his family, by the sole authority of a man called doctor superintendent.

A very intelligent patient told me once: "This is a damnable institution, wherein the husband is kept separated from his wife, and the wife kept separated from her husband." (literally). And in fact we have known in the sole ward 9 S two patients, men of more or less good sense and reason, who declared both of them, that they were detained in the hospital for the sole reason that their wives did not want them at home. One of them after having been detained here for about twenty months, was liberated (May '86) exactly in the same state of mind that he was when we saw him admitted for the second time, about eleven months before. The other had been in the hospital for seven years, I think, and he may be there yet. And does not the late case of Charles R. Brainerd prove, in its way, the necessity of investigation in the matter of wrong detention of persons in insane hospitals? If reform is not needed in this direction, I don't see where reform is needed.

CHAPTER X.

TRANSFORMATION—HOW TO SPEND THE MONEY?

Now while such is the real cause of insanity—Satan*—
and consequently that it is impossible for the doctor of
medicine to remove it and cure a single case, it is here,
citizens, the reform must bear.   Listen: $4,600 are now
annually paid, for instance, for the doctors' salaries of the
Northern hospital, without a single case of insanity or
epilepsy cured by them, given in return for your money.
Therefore you may, nay, you must, save that money to
employ it in a way to surely relieve and cure the patients.

In like manner, while it is impossible to show, that the
members of the board of supervision have ever caused the
cure or even the relief of a single patient, employed by
the state—by the people—at the enormous salary of
$10,000 annually.

While they have not hindered the patients being cruelly,
wretchedly treated right along.

While they have not hindered the making of three different kinds of board.one for the doctors and high officers.a
second for the employes of second class, and a third one for
the patients, who are fixed a part of the time with bread
and water, instead of ordering a good, substantial board
equal for all, according to the simplest principles of
equality and equity.

Whereas they have not made a single one of the pressing,necessary,indespensable reforms spoken of in this book.

That, if they have made some reparations or
improvements in, and around the buildings, and in

---

*We have found by God's grace and light, the AUTHOR of insanity and ep-
ilepsy. It is the devil. If any accused person before any honest jury had
such testimonies against him, he would be surely pronounced guilty.

the yard, that profits nothing to the patients, while they are no better fed, nor clothed, nor treated, nor sooner healed.

Then you may again, nay! you must retire the money allowed to them for supervision of the insane hospitals, at least, and employ that money in a way to relieve and cure some patients.

Now how to spend usefully, in behalf of the patients, those thousands of dollars, spent now uselessly, and without benefit to the insane, is the question. After having been almost four months insane in the Northern hospital, and having remained therein for over fourteen months after my recovery, examining all things, every day at will, I do really believe that God has enabled us thereby, to see how that money may be usefully spent for the good and cure of the patients. Then, please, listen: You must put in each ward a sufficient number of good, devoted christians to attend to the mental, moral, and spiritual as well as the physical needs of the patients. Under the present administration, two or three attendants* are placed in each ward to take care of about thirty-five patients: three attendants in the wards of the most insane generally, and two of them in the wards of more intelligent patients. But we have shown you how the insane are treated by them. They tried to quiet the patients by blows, strangulations, opiates and sundry punishments, and they strapped down and handcuffed the violent and even the noisy patients, and worse yet.† (And eat the good things while the patients are deprived of them.) That is 'the way I have been strapped down almost continually during the

---

At the time of our last visit to the hospital we found that they had increased the number of attendants, and placed two of them in the front wards, three in the middle wards, and four in the back wards.

†In St. Peter asylum we have found an unfortunate tightly strapped down on his bed by the upper part of the body. Then he had his two feet strapped down to the foot of the bed. Then each one of his hands strapped on each side of him. What sane man could keep his reason thus fixed?

three weeks of my last folly, though there was not the least bit of violence towards others, about me, at the time. But now we have demonstrated by real, living, existing facts, that such treatment renders the patients more crazy, and may kill them instead of healing them. No question about it. Satan don't cast out Satan. The thief come not, but for to steal and to kill and to destroy. But Christ came to save, to heal, to give life. Well then, this is our advice of reform—transformation, in this direction. Instead of two, three or four, rough attendants—actuated by the evil spirit—placed in each ward for about thirty-five patients, I would advise to place, in each ward for such number of patients, six, seven and eight attendants—animated by the Spirit of Christ—and this should be their task. Thus, every attendant should have only five or six patients, and only two or three, if violent or boisterous, under his care, and always the same patients for a certain time at least. Every attendant should have his own patients to take care of. With such a small number of patients, these christian attendants instead of beating, strangling, and strapping them down to quiet them as they do now, they should be always and under all circumstances, the best friends of the patients, soothing and calming them through kindness when irritated or disorderly. And those attendants, paid to behave this way towards the patients, should *have* to do it, or be discharged. Of course it should be expected that those christian attendants, would behave that way and perform all their other duties towards the patients, for the love of God and their insane brethren, more than because the laws of the institution should require it. If any being is worthy of compassion, it assuredly is the person bereaved of reason! What we rather need, citizens, in our insane asylums for attendants

are persons animated with the Spirit of Christ, devoted to
their brethren and sisters, the patients, as those missionaries, who, after having renounced the enjoyments of this
world, go at the risk of their lives to preach the gospel to
the heathen.—But again, with such a small number of patients, each of those new attendants should be personally
well acquainted with every patient under his care. He
should try to discover what is the moral character of his
patients as far as possible, their education, previous living,
occupation, surroundings, etc. And specially, what is the
delusion, or false idea, under which the patient labors, and
try to eradicate it every time from the patient's mind, by
a wise, kind and sympathetic reasoning to the level of the
patient's intellect.* And above all, in all cases, endeavor, so far as possible, to displace in the patient,
the evil spirit, and re-place it by the good Spirit of
God. This is the real cure of insanity, established on real,
living facts, and confirmed by the word of God. Listen:
Last winter (1886-7) while attending a holiness meeting
of the Salvation Army, in Minneapolis, there arose a man
who declared himself to be an extraordinary being, a man
of prophecy. At the close I spoke to the man, and I easily found out, that he labored under the delusion that he
was himself the great predicted Anti-christ, and consequently could not be saved. Here it is evident, that the
man was on the best possible way to an insane asylum. Now
suppose that his folly had manifested itself, and that he
had been taken to an insane hospital, there, the doctors
most probably would have given him some medicines to
drink, some novels or history to read, invited him to attend dances, card and checker plays, and so forth. Now
here, addressing myself to the people's common sense, I do

---

*Dr. C. E. Booth agreed completely with us upon the efficacy of this moral
treatment.

ask, Is it not evident that none of those hospital appliances could ever rid the patient's mind of the false idea that
troubled him, and that he might have remained all his
life therein without receiving any benefit from such foolish treatment? But some of the brethren explained to
the deluded man, with great charity, thank God, that the
predicted Anti-christ, must be, according to the Scriptures,
a prince, a king, a great monarch of the earth, and probably issu from some royal family, and that he, being a
simple workingman, was not and could never be the predicted Anti-christ, but that he was only deluded by the devil.
And they urged him to give God his heart, and accept
Christ for his Saviour and follow Him. And thank God
the man is still at large, striving to serve God.*

What we must know, before and above any thing else, in
this matter, is, that the insane has the *mind* troubled, affected generally, not the body. It is then his *mind* that must
be relieved, purged if possible of the delusion that troubles
him. The medicine of the doctor that goes down in the
stomach, and which is after cast out into the draught,
cannot attain this result, even should the medicine act
more or less on the blood, yet the blood is matter, and the
part affected is the mind, and sentiment. The doctor may
purge the bowels, and cleanse the blood of the patient, all
the year round, and not relieve his mind a particle. But
reasoning charitably applied in time may relieve the patient.† In fact if the patient, as we have established it to be

*Now Dr. Cyrus K. Bartlett of St. Peter asylum is in Europe for three
months or more. When the asylum may be run three months or more without a doctor superintendent, where is the man bold enough to venture to say
it could not be run that way all the year round? But now we say more than
this: Remove again the two assistant doctors and run the hospital by a
good, honest, christian superintendent, not a medical man, and you'll see
that not one case less will be cured, because the cause of the trouble here is
such that no doctor can remove it.

†That the insane, of course, very often will not listen, we must expect, because in many cases the insane do not see things as a sane person does,
and also in many cases, they have, for the time being, the hearing and some
other senses affected. But if some can't or will not actually listen, it is cer-

the case, has his mind troubled by some false ideas, implanted by the spirit of error and evil, to deliver him completely, radically, from his delusion, preach to him the Word of the Almighty God that cannot lie nor contradict itself, and give him this good word of truth to read, and inspire him with some taste and attachment for the reading of this good word, and we believe that any insane, that shall receive in his mind, and heart this word of truth shall be healed. It has healed me anyhow. Listen: The patient has the mind troubled by the spirit of Satan and all it takes to cure him is the Word which emanates from the Spirit of God. Or rather what it needs is the Word itself, the living Word, the Word made flesh—Jesus Christ. It takes the Christ to cast out Satan. Don't you know that it is in the name of Jesus Christ that one casts out the devil? Dost thou now understand my brother, the real remedy for insanity, madness, folly, mental alienation, craziness, lunacy and falling sickness, and of whatever name thou mayst call it, is Jesus Christ. Yes, Jesus Christ, I say. Replace the spirit of Satan that has taken possession of the mind and heart and will of thy brother, by the Spirit of the Lord Jesus Christ, and thy brother is saved, and gloriously delivered from his folly and blindness! Glory be to Jesus! And thou, fellow citizen, dost thou comprehend now all the folly of the doctors who refuse to the r patients, under pretext that it may hurt them, this Word of God, pure, perfect, sure, sweet, precious, living and piercing, and permanent forever, this two-edged sword of the spirit, this Word given and fulfilled by Jesus Christ, this unerring Guide, able to render wise unto salvation through faith in Christ, profitable to teach, to convince, to c rrect and to

---

tain that we cannot hurt them thereby. And surely it would be a great improvement in insane hospitals, if they only use therein such appliances cannot hurt the patients.

instruct according to righteousness, this Word intended to regenerate, enlighten, illuminate, to convert the soul, to sanctify and purify the heart, intended to deliver from the path of destruction, and to comfort and rejoice our hearts, the Word by which we must prove all things, which is a lamp to our feet, and a light in our path? and who want to relieve and cure the insane with novels, dances, card and checker plays, the pushing of swabs, drawing of sand bags, and with ice bags, cold packs, with some medicine as opium, morphia, phosphorus, hyosciamia, strychnia, etc., etc., and with electricity, etc.   And does it not seem to thee, just tell me, that here the folly of the doctors exceeds the folly of the patients?   And is not this the case, "the greatest fool of the two is not the one we thought."   And art thou yet surprised that with all such treatment many patients take the door that leads to the cemetery, rather than the door that should lead them towards their homes?

Error in a person's mind is far from always bringing insanity.   But insanity is always based on some error. Now the soil (the mind) where such seed (delusions or false ideas) may grow must be changed, renewed of course. And casting the devil and delusions out of the patient's mind, and re-placing them by the Word and Spirit of God, is the renewing process.   There is none other.   Thus the remedy we advise, visibly strikes the evil at the root.   No medicine, no doctor's appliance can do it.   Therefore, the mental, moral and spiritual treatment of insanity above described is alone adequate to effect a cure of this mental trouble.   The trouble is mental, moral, spiritual, and it takes the application of a mental, moral, spiritual treatment to overcome it.   No question about it.   *Medecin,* and medicines have nothing to do here in the generality of cases.   Peter, Philip, Paul cured permanently the possessed of devils, (the insane) by the Word of God, through faith. Doctors could not cure them then. The same trouble, produced by the same cause—Satan—most certainly demands now the same remedy. No question about it.

Wherefore in this way should be spent the money in behalf of the insane, by treating them, mentally, morally, and spiritually, by faithful disciples of the One who has said to the evil spirit: "Hold thy peace and come out of him." But brethren citizens, when you pay thousands of dollars annually to doctors and members of the board of supervision, that profit nothing to the insane, their troubled mind is not improved thereby, and they are none the less wretchedly treated. This I have seen during the eighteen long months of my detention in the Northern Wisconsin hospital.

Now however strange may appear to some persons our advice, to dispense, to the greatest extent possible, with that costly ministration of M. D's. in our insane hospitals, is nevertheless in perfect accordance with real, living, existing facts. Not only have we shown that while ready to die in the hands of three doctors of an insane hospital, themselves acknowledging it, a single passage of the Scriptures of truth, led me back permanently to reason, and we may cite some other cases of idiocy and madness cured by prayer alone ; but yet when it is evident that two or three times more cases are cured at Gheel, where the patients are taken care of by simple countrymen, (and where the most of incurable cases are received,) than in the Northern Wisconsin hospital, and when it is acknowledged by the doctors that more patients are cured in hospital receptacles as the ones of New Zealand quoted by Dr. P. Earle from the Journal of Mental Science, without doctors or medicines (their superintendents being not medical men) than generally in the best insane hospitals in England and United States if such living facts don't proclaim aloud, the powerlessness of the M. D's. to cure insanity, and that we should spend the money in favor of the insane in a better way than for doctors in medicine, then I declare that I do not understand anything in the usual language. Such observation is applicable, no doubt to the salary paid entirely uselessly to the members of the board of supervision. Yes, and if any man will contest this, let him show how the presence of the members of that board, in the hospital's office. or around the hospital, or abroad, may relieve the troubled mind of the patients. That's the way to do business.

Now brethren citizens don't you believe that I am a hater of the M. D's. or of the members of the board of supervision, because we speak in this way. No, thanks be to God, we have "charity for all and malice towards none." But after our experience and sojourn of eighteen months in the Northern hospital, I have certainly seen that in using the money paid uselessly to the above named gentlemen (doctors and members of the board) in the hiring of a great number of good, devoted, competent christian attendants, as explained above, would certainly relieve, and most probably cure a great number of our unfortunate brethren. And then on the other hand, those doctors relieved of a charge where they certainly can do no good. could employ their time and talents to treat perhaps successfully some bodily disease, and thus render some service to society and humanity, instead of staying in the insane asylums to be laughed at by the devil, the author and true cause of insanity, that they certainly cannot remove by the appliances of their blind science, and laughed at by all those who will henceforth know the true cause of the trouble.

And the same observation is applicable to the members of the board of supervision who could probably employ also their time and talents in some better way than to mingle themselves with the insane business in which they are utterly blind and can do no good.

Then I would also advise to hire so far as practicable, some good, faithful disciples of Christ from any denomination filled of faith and Holy Ghost, to go and preach to the insane, Jesus Christ, the great Deliverer from the power of Satan, in all the insane asylums, and we believe that every insane converted to Christ, would be restored to reason. It cannot be otherwise. Moreover, the Lord Jesus Christ has given the power to his disciples to cast the devils out of the possessed. And since Jesus Christ is the same yesterday, to-day and forever, I do not hesitate to believe that some may receive, in our days, the power to really cast the demons out of the insane in the name of the Lord Jesus Christ and permanently cure them thereby.

But to return to the attendants question and so forth. In setting in the wards 6, 7 and 8 attendants, instead of the actual number 2, 3 and 4, this would make an increase of 4 attendants in each ward, which multiplied by the number of 28 wards, males and females, would make an increase of 112 attendants for the whole building. And in paying each one of them a yearly salary of $400 (including the cost of their board) it would require a sum of $44,800 to pay them annually. Now we contend that for the half of the actual cost of maintenance, the patients could be fed and clothed better than they are now. And as this cost of maintenance amounts now to $167 per patient in the Northern Wisconsin hospital, this would make a reduction of $83.50 per patient which sum multiplied by the actual number of 600 patients would amount

to $50,100.   This sum would cover all the salaries of
the 112 new proposed attendants and leave a small surplus.   Then it would be advisable to appoint over the attendants a good, honest. christian superintendent, (not a
medical man) with a small salary, since all the needed
care would be taken by the attendants.   Medicines and all
such medical appliances should generally be prohibited in
insane asylums in treatment of insanity.   If any visible
physical cause of trouble exists in any patient, as a frac-
tured skull, any limb broken. etc., we won't say not use a
surgeon, or physician in such cases.   At any rate, if any
doctor, with a small salary, would be yet attached to the
insane institutions,   let it be well understood that this
physician should have nothing to do with the running of
the institution.   For we judge that medical science has
wronged and maltreated enough our insane to take them
out of its hands now.   To see whether a patient is completely restored to reason or not, the most expert will always be the devoted and intelligent attendant who is in
daily, hourly intercourse with him.   Then, as soon as it
is seen that a patient may be trusted at large on furlough,
the best way is to try him outside.   And if he fails to behave, take him back into the asylum.   Proper food strict-
ly equal for all, patients, employes and managers, should
be prepared and distributed, save only in cases of sick or
infirm patients who require a special diet.   No patient
should ever be set to work. except the one who himself
asks to work.   And if any patient is doing a useful,
necessary work, let him be paid for his labor.   Oh! woe!
woe! to the man or set of men, if they don't repent, who
have inaugurated the system of paying enormous salaries
to doctors and trustees to do nothing, or a useless work to
say the least, and keep working all the year around our
unfortunate brethren, the patients, and give them nothing

for their labor!! A board of supervision is more than
useless here. Not only there is no need at all of them,
but they might hinder the good work going on. If sometimes repairs or improvements are needed in or around the
buildings, call an honest architect to look at it and attend
to the work. Such is an outline of the reforms or transformation that should be effected in our insane asylums.
Some amendments might be made of course according to
the dictates of common sense, necessity, circumstances or
increase of light on this great question.

Thus it seems clear to us that without an increase of
expenses, the insane could be better fed, better clothed,
and receive the proposed mental, moral, and spiritual
treatment that would, we believe, cure a great number of
them.* And then right here, the benefit would be ten-
fold. Not only this surplus of recoveries would diminish in
proportion the expenses for insane, but how estimate the
good, joy and happiness resulting from the restitution to
their families and business, to society and liberty of the
number of patients owing their recovery to this new
mode of treatment? Citizens, let us try this new plan of
taking care of the insane. I know it will work and be
good and beneficial. It has in its favor good common sense,
experience in insanity, and the approbation of God's word.
Let us hope it will obtain also the approbation of any fair
minded person who has no personal interest to see the
present disastrous state of affairs continue in our insane
asylums. And it is at least certain that the only thing in
the view of him that advises this mode of treatment of
the insane, is the good, relief, deliverance, cure and salvation of those unfortunates; otherwise we have no benefit whether our plan be adopted or rejected. And it goes

* Money enough is spent in behalf of the insane. Only it needs badly to be
spent in the right way so that it profits them.

without saying that if this plan of treatment be good in the Northern Wisconsin hospital, it will be good in Madison, in St. Peter, in Rochester, and all over the land.

But brethren citizens, by the way, the devil is crafty, is he not? For centuries he certainly rendered insane our fathers, mothers, brothers, sisters, and wives and husbands, our children and friends, and then he caused us to send them to be healed to some doctors, visibly animated by his spirit, and who are his servants. And there of course, Satan casts not Satan out. For we have seen what they do with the insane and how they treat them. So Satan laughs at us. And such is the trick he plays on us since the foundation of our insane hospitals! And neither our pastors nor doctors have perceived it! Oh! what a diabolical trick!!*

But it is well for you O men and women (to me first) because the light has come and we have preferred the darkness! Read now only one of the four gospels, my brother, my sister, and you shall certainly see that the Lord Jesus Christ, the Creator of the body and soul and mind, attributed positively insanity and epilepsy to the power of the devil and evil spirits; and that to deny it one must have the mind blinded by Satan, as our brethren, the Universalists and the doctors of insane hospitals! And how is it possible that no one of us, my friends, neither pastors nor doctors, has had understanding on this question? But eighteen centuries ago Jews and Gentiles knew so well that insanity was caused by the power of the evil spirit that they were saying of a man they thought to be insane, or wanted him to be regarded as insane: "He hath a demon, and is out of his senses; why hear ye

---

* Wherefore let us hasten now to get Satan cast out of the insane in the name of Christ through faith, prayer, and by the preaching of the Word!

him?" Others said, "These are not the words of a demoniac? Can the demon open the eyes of the blind?"* And we did not see it! We knew it not! Blind that we are! Oh! it is true of you O men that it is written: "I will destroy the wisdom of the wise, and will bring to nothing the understanding of the prudent. Where *is* the wise? Where *is* the scribe? Where *is* the disputer of this world? Hath not God made foolish the wisdom of this world? For after that in the wisdom of God, the world by wisdom knew not God, it pleased God by the foolishness of preaching to save them that believe." Yes, and we may say, because the world by human wisdom could not find what was and is the true cause of insanity, it has pleased God to reveal it to a poor, ignorant insane—in order that he, himself, could not boast to have found it—"because the foolishness of God is wiser than men; and the weakness of God is stronger than men . . . . . . But God hath chosen the foolish things of the world to confound the wise; and God hath chosen the weak things of the world to confound the things which are mighty; and base things of the world, and things which are despised, hath God chosen, yea, and things which are not, to bring to naught things that are: That no flesh should glory in his presence."

Now, brethren, citizens, I believe I have done my duty in showing up and unveiling many things hidden in the darkness. Will you do yours? God grant you may. And may the God of peace and light lead and direct you, to bring about relief and deliverance to our brethren, the insane. Their relief, deliverance. cure and salvation, is all the reward I covet down here for my work, though poor, ignorant, without resources, it took me over two years of work, more or less assiduous, to write two editions

---

*John X 20, 21, (French translation.)

of this book, one in French and the other in English. And now, though we believe the work to be a very useful and necessary one, yet, as to style, we consider it as a poor literary production, and full of faults and defects.

Then I had to sell the inheritance of my father in Belgium to get the book published at my expense. But never mind. May only God bless this work of our hands, in relieving and delivering our brethren and sisters, the insane, out of the hands of the wolves that devour them, through Jesus Christ our Lord, the good Shepherd of the sheep!

And blessing, and honor, and glory, and power, be unto him that sitteth upon the throne, and unto the Lamb for ever and ever. Amen.

FRANCIS DELILEZ.

Minneapolis, June 1888.